Ethical Competence and Professional Associations

Andrew Friedman

ISBN: 978-0-9545487-7-3

Contents

List of figures and tables

Figures

Tables

List of case studies

Acknowledgements

Much of the material in the second part of this book is based on comprehensive surveys of professional associations carried out in 2006 and in 2003. We would like to thank all the professional associations in the UK and Ireland who took the time to answer what was a very long and detailed questionnaire. We would especially like to thank those that agreed to be interviewed for case studies.

There are many staff at PARN who have contributed to this book. I would like to thank Emily Pickering, Polly Procter and Natasha Price for carrying out and preparing case studies for this book. I would also like to thank Christina Williams and Jane Mason for their work on the design of the questionnaire and for support with editing this book, Xiaojie (Lin) Kirby for her work on the cover design and especially Nataliya Afitska for providing the quantitative analysis of the surveys on which the tables in this book are based. Finally I would like to thank Julia Denman for general support for the book and particularly for organising and carrying out the final proof reading and style checking.

Preface

This is the third book on professional ethics to be produced by the Professional Associations Research Network (PARN). The first (Friedman, Phillips and Timlett, 2002) was based on 52 professional codes collected during 2000 and 2001 as well as presentations and comments made at a workshop on professional ethics held in February 2002. In that book the following aspects of professional codes were explored.

1.   Labels given to the code - Code of Ethics, code of conduct

2.   Structure of the code - size and level of detail

3.   Language used - degree of compulsion implied by individual statements in the code

4.   Values and principles - the nature and 'meaning' of the particular obligations specified

5.   Stakeholders - to whom are the particular obligations owed, and how are stakeholders involved in the development and promotion of the codes

6.   Enforcement and support for the codes - complaints and disciplinary procedures, positive supports through education.

The second book (Friedman, Daly and Andrzejewska, 2005) was confined more narrowly to the Ethical Codes themselves. Seventy codes were examined during 2004 and early 2005. At the heart of that book was a model in which three of the themes of the first book (language; values and principles; and stakeholders – labelled beneficiaries in that second book) were developed and combined as three dimensions of a 'Matrix'. The aim was to establish a way of describing and analysing codes that captures these complex aspects in a robust manner; not only for others to be able to replicate the findings, but also to allow other professional codes to be analysed and compared rigorously. Work on the 'Matrix' was used to help develop principles to guide the writing and revision of codes. Principles of accessibility, clarity, and consistency were developed and illustrated. The key advantage of using the 'Matrix' is that once a particular code is plotted onto it, one instantly is presented with a structured view of what is missing from that code (at least compared with the 70 codes that were used to create the 'Matrix'). One recommendation was that to whom particular obligations are owed should be explicit in the code. Also it was recommended that the code be regarded as a public document and not only as an internal support for initial training of professionals or merely a part of the procedures for disciplining them. Accessibility was identified in terms of number of 'clicks' required to reach the code from the association's homepage.

Ethical Competence and Professional Associations differs from the other two books in that it is focused on Ethical Codes as part of a constellation of activities developed by professional bodies in order to support and encourage what we have labelled the ethical competence of professionals. Also this book deals, at least in passing, with a subject of several other PARN books, that is, continuing professional development (CPD). Ethical competence can be thought of as the outcome of joining professional ethics with professional education and development. We define it as a step beyond technical competence. In the first chapter ethical competence is defined carefully and related to definitions of professionalism. Its importance to society, to professionals and to professional associations is discussed. In the remaining chapters of the first part of this book we explore the concept of ethical competence from several different angles. First we examine the component parts of the phrase ethical competence separately. Chapter 2 discusses ethics and professional ethics. Chapter 3 deals with competencies and competence. In Chapter 4 we put ethical competence together and consider the foundations and the components of ethical competence. We then look at the process of acquiring ethical competence. This involves incorporating other aspects of professionalism: technical competence and reflective practice in particular, but it also concerns a distinction developed in Chapter 3 between competencies and competence and their relation to effective performance and the likelihood of future effective performance. We also briefly distinguish phases in the process of exercising ethical competence

The second part of this book deals with supports for ethical competence that professional associations can provide and are providing. Evidence for the supports that are being provided is presented based on comprehensive surveys of professional associations carried out by PARN in the UK and Ireland in 2003 and 2006. Examples of interesting and good practice on these subjects are presented in a series of case studies. This empirical base of information on the activities of professional associations is described and evaluated briefly in an appendix. Chapter 5 examines the direct supports for Ethical Codes. Chapter 6 deals with education supports both in terms of initial professional qualifications and continuing professional development. Chapter 7 deals with what may be labelled remedial supports for ethical competence, that is, complaints and disciplinary procedures. The book ends with a brief chapter on conclusions and recommendations.

PARN is a 'research-enriched network' and a membership organisation with 150 members comprising professional bodies in Australia, Canada, Ireland and the UK. PARN carries out and publishes research, holds networking events, and provides advice to its members on subjects of concern to professionals and particularly to professional bodies. Substantial work has been carried out since 1998 on: continuing professional development, governance and management of professional bodies, member relations and member services, organisation strategy, internationalisation of professional bodies, in addition to work on Ethical Codes and ethical competence.

The PARN website (www.parn.org.uk) provides information on these subjects as well as other PARN activities.

- Part 1 -
Understanding ethical competence and its relation to professionalism

- Chapter 1-
What is ethical competence and why is it important?

1.1   Introduction

In this chapter we introduce the concept of ethical competence and consider the connection between it and the overall concept of a profession or professionalism. We also examine the specific ways ethical competence can be understood and describe the way it will be used in this book. We then examine the importance of ethical competence, for society, for professionals and for professional associations.

1.2   Defining ethical competence

Ethical competence can mean different things depending on which of the two words is emphasised and whether ethical refers to theoretical or practical ethics.

We interpret ethical *competence* as a type of competence that allows us to distinguish between skill or expertise or technical competence, and professionalism. It is the exercise of competence in an ethical manner; it is a practical accomplishment. It will not reside with an individual who desires to become a professional before that person acquires an understanding of the knowledge and technical basis for the profession and experiences professional practice or at least a simulation of professional practice as part of training for a profession. It is different from, more than, a facility with common morality; with adhering to the ethical norms of society. Professional ethical competence builds on professional technical competence, but it is different from it. Ethical competence highlights an extra element that should be added to expertise in order for an expert to qualify as a professional; it concerns the manner in which expertise is exercised and qualified in order to encourage trust. Thus ethical competence is a way, we suggest one of the most important ways, of distinguishing a practitioner as a professional.[1]

For professionals ethical competence may be more concretely defined as the ability to carry out the activities or practice of an occupation in a manner as defined by Ethical Codes of conduct (and other guidance documentation and advice) promulgated through professional associations. This generally involves knowing when to apply and when to forbear from applying knowledge, based on ethical principles: what is 'right' and not 'right' taking into account client needs as well as what is morally correct and sensitive to the situation of clients and other stakeholders.

It also involves knowing how to perform professional services in a manner beyond that which is precisely prescribed by the Ethical Codes of professional associations. It also concerns knowing how to react to situations in the 'spirit' of the codes. Here is where guidelines and advice and more substantial educational materials provided by the association or provided by third party suppliers accredited by the association, are relevant.

A second way of interpreting the phrase *ethical* competence is competence at ethics. This could mean competence at theoretical ethics, an accomplishment that might be expected of a philosophy graduate. It could also mean expertise at identifying the public interest, public good or the frontiers of professional ethics, someone who is especially attuned to ethical considerations of actions. Someone who is ethically competent in this sense could, for example, be a person who has studied the Human Rights Act and reflected on its implications, someone who is aware of the precedents by which the disciplinary committee of a professional association currently operates. Such people can be extremely useful if their services are organised by a professional association to support the membership, say through ethics telephone helplines or as part of ethics committees. These ways of thinking of *ethical* competence supplement our treatment of the term here. In order to avoid confusion, we reserve the term *ethical competency* for the interpretation in this paragraph of what might otherwise be regarded as ethical competence. The difference between competency and competence is primarily that competency concerns a

---

[1] There is another broad concept that is arguably equally important a mark of the professional. This is reflective practice. The relationship between reflective practice and ethical competence is discussed in Chapter 4.

narrow, specialist subject or activity and primarily addresses the ability to execute a set of techniques or behaviours which are packaged up into that narrow subject or activity. Competence is broader and involves mastery not only of what techniques or activities are involved, but also judgement as to what elements of a broad repertoire are needed in order to carry out the activity effectively. It concerns when to apply the techniques and when to either apply other techniques from a broad repertoire of possibilities, or when to forbear from applying a certain broad set of techniques all together. This distinction between competency and competence, and how it relates to professionalism and to ethical competence, are dealt with in detail in Chapter 3.

We must also distinguish professional ethical competence from competence at ethical aspects of other social behaviour. Professional ethical competence can be defined quite clearly from formal documents and specific activities which define and support ethical competence of professionals, through the collective effort of professional associations and regulatory bodies. Norms for other forms of social activity are generally more diffuse. Some forms of social activity have clearer definitions of ethical competence, such as certain social clubs like the boy scouts and girl guides. Others are less clear, such as sports clubs and the behaviour of fans at sporting events. Ethical competence in certain aspects of social life are widely diffused, such as the norms of casual social intercourse in public (though the formulation of policies on anti-social behaviour orders or ASBOs is arguably making norms by which one can recognise ethical competence in encounters between neighbours and in the public streets around pubs and nightclubs much clearer). Ethical competence in these situations is, however, open to different interpretations, if one takes into account the ethical norms of street gangs compared with parents of young children living in those neighbourhoods, or the local police. Other aspects of social behaviour are also clearly divided, such as the expectations of ethical competence when making private investments.[2] While there may in fact be a gap between the aspirations for ethical competence expressed in professional Ethical Codes and the norms of ethical behaviour of certain professionals, as well as between the aspirations expressed in those codes and the

---

[2] There are certain groups that define their investment offerings to the public as socially responsible investments or ethical investment trusts. Private investors who would only use such vehicles may consider themselves to be ethically competent, but not all investors would agree. Rather, using the distinction noted above, we would consider them to have an ethical competency rather than being ethically competent (see Friedman and Miles, 2001).

expectations of clients and the general public, there are clear mechanisms which can continually act to reduce these gaps. These mechanisms, both positive support for Ethical Codes and remedial actions for those that transgress codes through complaints and disciplinary procedures, distinguish professional ethical competence from ethical competence at other forms of social interaction. However we strongly believe that these mechanisms must not be taken for granted. They are as necessary for the definition, maintenance and value of professional ethical competence as the existence of professional codes of conduct.

1.3 Meanings of professionalism in relation to ethical competence

To be a 'professional' can mean many things. One definition of professional is merely to be paid for your work, to be a professional as opposed to an amateur. This distinction then relates to giving the job one's full attention, taking it seriously. For most, being a professional means being qualified, through a process that involves education and training, in order to carry out some occupation. Another and related view of being a professional concerns autonomy and trust. Professional practice cannot be managed by direct control; it is generally too complex, too uncertain in outcomes and requires too much judgement and background expertise for the activities involved to be specified in advance and directed in minute detail. To be professional in these senses means having expertise, and in addition, it means being trusted to exercise that expertise in a responsible manner. This is the sense in which we regard professional here. This is the base assumption behind the identification of professionalism with ethical competence.

Professionals are expected above all to perform to a standard of competence. They are presumed to perform as though they have mastered the field of knowledge and techniques that characterise their profession. This includes an expected recognition of what knowledge and techniques are needed to meet the service requirements of their clients or their employers. It is here that ethical competence comes in. Not only are professionals expected to be technically competent, able to perform the services expected of them to a sufficient degree of competence, they are also expected to take care in the manner in which the services are delivered, and particularly they are expected to

22

use their professional (client interest-centred) judgement as to which services they should deliver and the manner of delivery. They are particularly expected to use their judgement to forbear from delivering a service they believe to be not ultimately in their client's interest (or at least to inform the client of this judgement). In this professionals are expected to be trustworthy.

A great deal of attention has been given in sociological literature to defining professional in order to distinguish clearly professional from non-professional occupations (Wilensky, 1964). We consider this to be misguided. Professionalism is what is important and professionalism is a matter of degree. Furthermore, professionalism is not a static state for any profession. It is a concept situated in history and supported by certain historically specific institutions and attitudes. It is in itself a changing concept, and more to the point, it is a concept that applies more or less to different occupations reflecting the time when activities emerged as full-time occupations and the actions taken by leading members of those occupations to professionalise. Many occupations are still professionalising, many have only recently begun to move along the path to professionalisation. Even the most traditional and long established professions are continually acting to support, maintain and develop their professionalism. Indeed for some, professionalism is in decline, though this is relatively rare.[3] Professionalism is therefore better thought of as a matter of degree and one that needs to be actively developed and maintained. At any moment in time it is better to think of a range of variation between more and less professionalised occupations, rather than a hard boundary between professional and non-professional occupations. It is also important to regard this range of variation as continually changing.[4]

---

[3] Public trust has declined towards certain professions, and they have come to be regarded as 'unprofessional'. Arguably this has been occurring in relation to politicians, encouraged for example by the 'cash for honours' accusations and by a reluctance of politicians to admit misdeeds or to resign when found to be acting to standards below what is expected of them. Even these examples represent a matter of degree and the consequent decline in professionalism can be reversed.

[4] The professions may be regarded as a 'system' characterised by competing claims of 'jurisdiction' over different fields of knowledge and practice (Abbott, 1988). While this approach provides some insight into the commonality of professions in their concern with fields of knowledge and practice, and discourages a static view of the traditional positions of different occupational groups within a structure of the 'sector of professional associations' (see Friedman with Afitska, 2007), Abbott's approach is itself too narrow. Open competition between professional groups is relatively rare and occupies only a small number of professional associations for limited periods of time.

Trustworthiness is also subject to a range of variation. Certainly it is less a matter of degree in relation to a single encounter between a particular client and a particular individual service provider. They are either trusted sufficiently for the client to accept the professional/client interaction, or they are not, and therefore thought trustworthy or not.[5] After the service encounter the result is either a maintained view on the part of the client that the professional they have been dealing with is trustworthy or not. This then can contribute to that client's view of the trustworthiness of that profession as a whole. The client's experience can also influence other potential clients and other stakeholders in their view of that individual practitioner and of that profession. The accumulation of service encounters, some of which may be regarded as unsatisfactory by some clients, even if the numbers are very small, can affect the overall view of the trustworthiness of that professional and that profession. Often this overall view will not reflect simple proportions of satisfied and unsatisfied clients. Some encounters will be more publicised than others, usually the unsatisfactory ones. The balance of satisfactory and unsatisfactory encounters with professionals will affect overall public perceptions, but these will also be strongly affected by other factors as well.

One set of factors affecting public opinion of the trustworthiness of a profession concerns the signals people accept as indicating both technical and ethical competence. Certification is important here as is the publicity given to Ethical Codes and the supports for ethical competence described in the second part of this book. However, a further important influence is mass media attention to various aspects of professional practice, and particularly to incidents of professional malpractice, which itself varies over time, particularly due to periodic 'media frenzies'. Therefore whether professions are viewed as trustworthy will depend on: the actual encounters clients have with them; the ethical competence of individual professionals; the supports for ethical competence provided by professional associations; and the balance of signals coming from other sources about the professions - primarily from the mass media, but also from government pronouncements and activities.

---

[5] Though even here trust can be a matter of degree in that the client may search for recommendations about the quality of the professional or try to protect themselves by more careful scrutiny of the service contract.

At the Professional Associations Research Network (PARN) we define professions using a simple definition. They are occupations where there is:

- An education and/or experience criteria for gaining membership into the profession and a system for maintaining standards and quality of service

- A code of conduct or ethical guidance for professional practice

- A commitment to continuing professional development

- An organisation that maintains a register of the members of the profession.

Defining professional as exercising professional ethical competence relates to the way PARN has defined professions in that Ethical Codes are part of the definition. All other aspects of the PARN definition of professions can be connected to ethical competence, and as we argue in this book, should be so connected. For example the education requirements, both in terms of initial professional qualifications and continuing professional development, need to be supportive of ethical competence and the Ethical Code as well as providing technical competencies and supporting overall technical competence. Courses and other forms of educating members of what ethical competence is and guidance on how it can be practiced ought to figure strongly in the role that professional associations play in supporting the very professionalism of their members.

The PARN criteria are not applied strictly in that PARN is concerned with professionalisation as well as professionalism. We generally accept organisations if they are definitely moving towards clear systems of entry standards and service quality standards, towards a code of conduct and a continuing professional development (CPD) policies and programmes. Some newly emerging associations have some but not all of these characteristics. The level of education standards, the rigor of the CPD policy and the substance of the CPD programme, as well as the quality of the Ethical Code and how substantial are the policies supporting the code, are all open to wide variations among professional associations.

1.4 Why is ethical competence important for society?

Ethical competence is a necessary accomplishment in all societies and especially for progress in what may broadly be called technology (the application of knowledge) because all knowledge has a degree of exclusiveness. There will always be "asymmetry of knowledge." This is because the person applying the knowledge will normally know more about what it is that they are doing (and 'should' be doing) than who they are doing it for (employer, direct supervisor, peers)[6] or to (client or patient or other employee). They will have a better understanding of whether the link between the knowledge and its application is correct, appropriate, likely to lead to an effective result, likely to generate negative collateral consequences and whether such consequences are likely to be significant in terms of the recipient's or other stakeholder's expectations of the activity or event. The more complex the task, the longer is the service encounter, and the less frequently the service encounter takes place the more pronounced this information asymmetry will be. These technical features of the 'supply' of certain services do not determine, by themselves, which services will be professionalized.

Professionalisation is not a technologically predetermined or 'natural' way of organising these occupations. They are not organised as professions in all countries and they certainly have not been organised as professions throughout the history of such occupations and similar occupations in countries where the professions are common today. Professionalism is an accomplishment, the result of a professionalisation project (Larson, 1977). It must be achieved by a set of agents acting in a strategic, a conscious and directed, manner. Some activities and occupations are 'easier' to professionalise. The opportunities to professionalise are not equally distributed across occupations. The technical factors mentioned above help to locate the smoothest lines, the paths of least resistance, to professionalisation. However, these characteristics are themselves not entirely inherent to particular occupations or activities. Occupations and activities can be made more complex or can be simplified, though these processes take time. We have been witnessing great changes in many occupations due to the influence of the Internet in the past decade. Also within service occupations there is a regular process of change due to the

---

[6] Unless of course they are working as a sole proprietorship practice.

commodification of some services and the hiving off of more complex and discretionary activities that are often taken on by other people arising from that commodification.

For example in the area of management consulting, certain forms of advice have become 'packaged up' and can be 'ordered' by those procuring consultancy (such as business process reengineering or reorganisation). Several companies offer rather similar packages. It becomes easier for procurement officers to develop contracts that specify what they want and this makes fixed price deals more possible. Certainly this does not obviate the need for a professional service to be supplied, even if the service has become more commodity-like. However the asymmetry of information becomes less severe between professional and client on this issue. As the product becomes more widely available a new situation arises whereby organisations need advice as to which product to choose and whether the product is needed at all, or whether organisations should be carrying out such exercises without outside consultancy help. More of a diagnostic sort of consultant is required, perhaps for shorter jobs, but jobs where information is highly asymmetric.

In addition to these supply factors, there are the demand factors; namely the importance to the client of the service offered. In all societies there will be certain services that are regarded as particularly important to recipients in terms of both how they are valued and the urgency with which they are needed. In addition there will always be services that have attached to them dire consequences for recipients if they receive what they regard to be inadequate services. It is here where the value of professionalism is most acutely felt.

Together these technical and social characteristics of certain services, activities or occupations identify those that are most likely to become most highly professionalised because these activities and occupations are ones where ethical competence is needed to bridge the information asymmetry gap and to reassure recipients that the outcome of the service encounter will be in line with their expectations. These are the areas where trust is needed and therefore they are the areas where assurances of ethical competence are more likely to lead to social support for professionalisation. Again, this is not to imply in a simple functionalist sense that if there is a need for ethical competence, professionalisation will be forthcoming in all instances as a natural consequence. Professionalisation is, as noted above, an accomplishment that requires determined effort by at least a section of practitioners.

The accomplishment of ethical competence by members of society is not perfect, it is a matter of degree. By and large most people are constrained to apply their knowledge in an ethical manner by the norms of society. Some would equate the norms of society as the ethical principles that are meant to guide social behaviour. However these norms do not form a strict 'template' for all behaviour. Some of these norms are imposed by structural features of society, by features that do not seem to rely on strategic or purposive actions of people. The forces of competition, based on the laws of contract (and tort) force people to behave in a manner which is expected, which does not transgress societal norms. However ethical competence is both a broad term that can be interpreted in different ways and it is a term for which there is considerable latitude, at least in some directions. Therefore ethical competence can be accomplished to different degrees, even when there is agreement about the norms.

In addition, what is expected of some people is different from that expected of others. While there is a common morality, certain people, particularly those in the professions and among them, those who are extremely public in their behaviour or those who can do great harm to clients and the general public if they do not behave according to those extra ethical elements, are either expected to adhere to the common morality more strictly, or are expected to adhere to a somewhat higher standard of morality.

Both competence and ethics are extremely broad concepts and there is a danger that the concept of ethical competence can become so diffuse that it would be difficult to recognise it or to recognise ethical *in*competence. This is mitigated when the concept is applied to professionals. Professional knowledge is defined as the field or 'jurisdiction' that the profession claims to occupy. Standards of technical competence are enshrined in the standards of initial professional qualifications awarded or accredited by a representative professional association, in conjunction with higher education institutions and other training providers. Standards of ethical competence are defined, or at least indicated, by codes of ethics and supporting guidelines and other materials produced and promulgated through the professional association.

Consider the following example, a health professional is asked to apply their knowledge in a particular manner, say by administering a health procedure such as a course of physiotherapy or chiropody. During the course of the treatment, the physiotherapist or chiropodist begins to question the value of the current course of treatment and begins to suspect that a different, more radical or expensive or invasive treatment may achieve better results. At what point should the professional call into question what they have been doing? Should they complete the course as originally agreed or recommended? Should they point out that extras are needed? Should they offer to carry out the extras? How many extras?

Where should we look for guidance on these matters? Is it not highly problematic if these matters are not settled, or at least clarified to the extent that people know what to expect when someone applies their knowledge to produce or convey something for another? If people do not know, or have a good reason not to trust, that an item they may purchase is any good, they are likely to expect the worst and act accordingly. This will drive prices down and may cause the market to collapse. No one would want the service because the market signals that no one trusts that it will be any good. If not the problem of the market for "lemons" occurs[7]. In this sense the market is no substitute for professional ethical competence. A minimal level of ethical competence is needed in order for markets to work at all.

Ethical competence is clearly an important accomplishment and a necessary one for the stability and sustainability of any society, though particularly one where people's sense of well being does not come from a single source, such as the state or the local warlord and where the knowledge base of society is complex and uncertain or changing. In these circumstances, without widespread ethical competence, one person would have little confidence in what they were going to get when they ask someone to do something for them, whether or not they pay for it to be done. They would have little confidence in whether they were getting as good a service as possible, whether they are being told of the reasons why they should consider not having the service or having alternative services, and what the consequences are likely to be of having the service carried out for them.

---

[7] Akerlof (1970) on Lemons - here lemons refer to second hand cars that are below standard.

1.5 Why is ethical competence important for professionals?

Professionals seem not to be trusted as much as they used to be. This is a commonplace these days. According to common parlance trust has not gone, but rather blind trust has been replaced by qualified trust. Trust needs to be earned or justified. Merely being a professional, wearing the white coat or putting a certificate up on the wall does not guarantee trust in a world where such a substantial proportion of the population has a university education, where a great deal of professional expertise can be accessed through the Internet, and where general deference to authority has declined.

At the launch of an RSA[8] project on professional values, Lord Phillips of Sudbury, warned that the "moral ozone layer" of the professions had become depleted through managerialism and the complexity of legislation and regulation. Professions will have to "get in trim" in order to develop the necessary moral fortitude for their very survival (Reece, 2002).

We contend that this can only occur if ethical competence is recognised as fundamental to the strength of the professions and to their importance in modern society. Arguably, the side of professionalism that is purely expertise, expertise at applying complex and difficult to understand theory, as well as highly specialised techniques to practical situations, without much concern for the ethical dimension involved, has come to dominate. This has led to a decline in trust in professionals. Professionals must become more aware of what is required for ethical competence, more careful in the manner in which they operate and more vigilant about practices among their colleagues which they regard as unethical.

Another problem is the formalisation of ethical competence into rules and procedures. This can be regarded as the antithesis of reliance on ethical competence, or it can be regarded as guiding behaviour in such a way as to avoid the likelihood of behaving in an ethically incompetent manner. Largely in relation to non-professionals, but also in relation to front line professionals like nurses and social workers, Neuberger (2006) despairs of "the moral state we're in" where individuals do not help others for fear of breaking rules or becoming vulnerable to legal

---

[8] Royal Society for the Encouragement of Arts, Manufactures & Commerce.

action. Ethical competence is not straightforward, it does not merely involve following rules.

While it is not likely that professions will ever return to a situation where the majority of the general public trusts them blindly, it is possible for some of the ground lost in recent years to be regained. How can professionals achieve this? We contend that it is not possible for professionals as individuals alone, to turn public opinion. Collective effort is required and the focus of such collective effort must be professional associations and related professional bodies.

1.6 Why is ethical competence important for professional associations?

Ethical competence will not be exercised at all times by all professionals. Instances of behaviour that falls below the ethical standard as set out in codes and professional norms must not be swept under the carpet. Unfortunately there is now a public perception that this has been the case for many years among many professions. The recent occurrence of explicit whistle-blowing clauses in codes of conduct reflects the view that peers often do not report breeches of the code. When they are reported in the past breeches have often been dealt with behind closed doors, without results becoming known, even to those directly affected. Furthermore there is a public perception that punishments are too light. The aim of the involvement of the professional body appears to the general public to be merely to protect individual members of the profession and to protect the reputation of the profession as a whole. We believe there are many things professional associations can do to improve ethical competence, not only in ensuring that members achieve the required standard of ethical competence, but also in terms of developing the theory and practice of ethical competence itself, that is, in developing and clarifying not only the way individuals can be brought up to the standard, but also in developing and clarifying the standard itself. However, we also believe that professional associations need to do more to show that they are encouraging a climate of ethical competence in their respective professions, which includes both positive supports for Ethical Codes and remedial action when codes are breeched. Overall ethical competence should represent a strategy professions pursue in order to improve their standing with the general public and the trust potential clients have in them.

Ethical competence, even as an ideal, has a historical dimension to it. That is, it is not an absolute. What practices are ethical can change over time. Also, it may be that as time goes on the way professional associations interpret and support ethical competence changes. The purpose of this book is not only to elucidate the concept of ethical competence because it is important for understanding what professional practice is. But it is also to draw attention to ethical competence in order to emphasise its importance for future practice. In a similar vein to Schön's (1983) elaboration of reflective practice, we believe that ethical competence has been rather underrated by the professions and that this leads to a reduction in the strength and influence of the professions as a whole.

Almost all professional associations have a Code of Ethics or a code of conduct which includes statements about obligations to the wider public. Unfortunately many associations do not make these obligations as clear as they could, codes are not written as consistently as they should be and codes are not as accessible to the public as possible (see Friedman et al. 2005). This is the challenge to professional associations that we believe many are now rising to. Chapters 5 to 7 of this book provide evidence that this challenge is being taken seriously by many professional associations in the UK and Ireland.

- Chapter 2 -
Professional ethics: the basis for professional codes of ethics

2.1   Introduction

Professional ethics can be defined by using codes of conduct published by various professional bodies as a guide. What is called the Ethical Code or code of conduct is usually a short document, only one or two pages long. It is often supplemented with guidelines, which are longer documents providing interpretation of the Ethical Code for specific circumstances. However what is included in any one code of a professional body may seem arbitrary compared with others. Some codes seem to reflect short term concerns affecting particular professional bodies, rather than foundational principles. One way of dealing with this has been attempts to devise overarching principles that can be used across all professions. For example the European Council of the Liberal Professions, are developing an 8-point set of principles they recommend to be included in all professional codes (see www.ceplis.org). Another approach is to develop a classification scheme that allows different professional codes to be compared on a consistent basis. This is the approach taken by PARN in the past (Friedman et al., 2005). We begin with a discussion of general attempts to define ethical behaviour, which are not limited to professionals, and then go on to examine professional codes.

2.2   General definitions of ethical behaviour

2.2.1   Ethics in philosophy

Philosophers deal with underlying principles or foundations for ethics. The main competing foundations are utilitarianism and Kantian deontological theory (see Beauchamp and Bowie, 2004).

Utilitarianism is particularly associated with Jeremy Bentham (1748-1832) and John Stuart Mill (1806-1873). According to utilitarianism ethical behaviour should be guided by the principle of utility: the greatest happiness or absence of pain or displeasure should determine right action (Mill, 1863). Bentham and Mill were hedonistic utilitarians, believing only that pleasure or happiness is intrinsically good. Everything else is good only to the extent that it leads to pleasure or away from pain. Later, pluralistic utilitarians, argued that other values had intrinsic worth such as beauty, courage, friendship, health and knowledge. Criticisms of utilitarianism are that some things may on balance give the greatest pleasure, but they offend other moral considerations, such as justice. Also utilitarianism is criticised because of the difficulty of comparing utility or preferences between people and this makes it is difficult to aggregate pleasures and pain across individuals.

Immanuel Kant (1724-1804) was concerned with motives for actions and in particular actions based on a recognition of the duty or moral obligation to act. The motive for action should be a person's 'good will' and this will be identified by a person's willingness to act according to the universal law of obligation; that is, one ought only to act in a way that one can also will that the maxim should become a universal law. This Kant took to be a "categorical imperative"; there are no exceptions. Examples Kant gave were not to lie, not to commit suicide, to help others in distress and to work to develop one's own abilities. Kantian ethics also incorporates the view that people should be treated as ends in themselves, and not as the means to the ends of others, unless they freely agree to it. Kantian ethics have been criticised for leaving out consideration of moral emotions such as sympathy or caring.

For utilitarians, consequences are most important; it is the act that matters.[9] For Kantians, motives and particularly the motive to follow moral rules are most important; it is the individual actor that is the focus. These theorists have traditionally sought a set of universal rules or principles that would allow those wishing to behave ethically to decide on the morally right actions to take in any particular case. They would also aim for such rules to be stated in such clear terms that anyone could understand and apply them correctly. Professional ethics as summarised in codes of conduct are clearly of a deontological

---

[9] There is a distinction between Act Utilitarians and Rule Utilitarians. Act Utilitarians allow for individuals to break moral rules if they lead to greater happiness over pain. They expect each situation to be judged according to the utilitarian principle. Rule Utilitarians believe that traditional moral rules will make it easier for most people to do the right thing on utilitarian grounds; will allow them to short-cut the need to calculate, as long as the rules have been shown by experience to have led to the greatest happiness.

nature. They set out rules for behaviour. However, many of the codes contain a set of moral characteristics or values that are difficult to acquire at the stage in life when people come to undergo training to acquire competence in a particular profession. Many would argue that these are character traits that are likely to have been acquired at a much younger age.

An alternative and growing philosophical tradition builds on this insight. It eschews a single foundational rule and instead enumerates a number of underlying characteristics or virtues that would make up an ethical person; that is, moral character. It could be argued that virtue ethics (Hursthouse, 1999) comes closer to the foundation for the ethics expressed in Ethical Codes of professional bodies. Virtue ethics is associated with Aristotle (384-322 BC/1999) and while it fell back as utilitarian and deontological ethics arose with the Enlightenment and particularly during the 19th century, virtue ethics has been revived in the past 50 years (Anscombe, 1958).

Aristotelian virtue ethics involves virtue (*arêta*), practical wisdom (*phronesis*) and well-being or happiness (*eudaimonia*). Virtues are deep character traits or dispositions to behave in certain ways that always, or almost always apply. The motive being that the characteristic is considered to be good in itself and not taken on because it is convenient or because it can lead to other desirable outcomes. It is likely to be accompanied by a deep emotional abhorrence at not following that virtue in oneself and also abhorrence on finding its absence in others. However there will be instances where virtuous behaviour is tested; where there are temptations to act otherwise. Here virtue ethicists distinguish between full or perfect virtue, where the virtuous one acts virtuously without a struggle, as opposed to continence or strength of will, where the virtuous person must struggle against a desire or temptation to act in a non-virtuous way. It is usually considered positive that one struggles against temptation to act in a non-virtuous way if that temptation is externally imposed, if it is due to difficult circumstances, rather than if it comes from a inner temptation to be non-virtuous, such as to act callously or dishonestly.

Virtuousness needs to be supported by practical wisdom. By taking each virtue on its own, it is possible that one can be motivated purely by emotion, without rational considerations. For example, one can be compassionate, motivated by observing the suffering of others, or one can show courage as fearlessness, willingness to face danger. These virtues, on their own, can lead to morally wrong actions. They indicate what Aristotle called natural virtue, which needs *phronesis* to be developed into its full potential. What is needed is an understanding of the circumstances one is acting in and of consequences of one's acts. For example by not assuming what suits oneself will be suitable for others.

There is a parallel here between the competencies-competence distinction (mentioned in Chapter 1 and elaborated in Chapter 3) and the distinction between virtue and practical wisdom. Various forms of specific skills or narrow forms of expertise are similar to virtues. On their own, in limited circumstances, the exercise of skills or specific competencies is necessary, valuable and probably sufficient. However, the exercise of one or other skill or form of expertise can lead to an unsatisfactory result if the circumstances of the exercise of that skill are not appropriate. It may, for example, be useful in the constrained situation of being employed to carry out a particular operation for an employer as ordered. The activity may be sufficient as it is specified in advance by that employer. However, if circumstances change there may be situations where the normal exercise of skill is inappropriate and may lead to a poor result. Generally only with practical experience can individuals recognise when it is important to refrain from exercising that skill, or to exercise it in a new way. This is a common complaint about the way individuals who have recently come out of higher education behave when they begin their apprenticeship or articles or other forms of practical training, or when fresh MBA graduates come to their first job. They want to apply what they have learned without understanding the limitations of the theories in real practical circumstances. Part of the problem is that the individual has only a narrow repertoire of learned actions. This repertoire needs to be broadened through experience. Part of the problem is the need for the individual to think through the consequences of the actions. Part of the problem is the need to actually find ways of forbearing from exercising the techniques as theoretically expected without seeming to shirk one's responsibilities, or feeling that one is shirking.

Generally this practical wisdom only comes with life experiences. And in essence what is often required is the ability to recognise that some features of a situation are more important or more relevant than others. Here we may see the difference between ethical competency and ethical competence. It is possible to know all the rules and even to know how to apply the rules. One may have studied the Ethical Code and all its guidelines. One may have worked through all kinds of moral dilemmas associated with the code. One may have passed exams on the subject and one may even be able to advise others as to what they should do in various circumstances. However, this is not the same as knowing what to do in particular circumstances one finds oneself in. It may not be enough to deal with conflicting senses of, or understandings of, obligations and to different stakeholders in the particular and perhaps emotionally charged situation one finds oneself in.[10]

Virtue ethics has been roundly criticised for not producing principles to guide action. However, if virtue ethics is supplemented by vice prohibitions, then the problem can be partially solved. A problem with virtue ethics is that relatively few virtues have been specified, but there is a longer list of vices to be avoided (Hursthouse, 1999). How do we decide which virtues will in fact lead a person to *eudaimon*, which ones make one responsive to the demands of the world in a manner that would allow one to be considered morally meritorious? Which ones are the characteristics of what would be generally considered to be a good person? There is clearly a problem if the list of virtues is radically different for different societies or groups in a society. One way that these problems can be, at least partially, addressed is if a community can come to an agreement on what virtues should apply to them and to publicise the list. That is, what is needed is a code that specifies the relevant virtues.

2.2.2   A general moral code

An approach that is close to one that may be used to assess and understand professional ethics, begins with what has been called common morality; that is, "the moral system that thoughtful people use, usually implicitly when they make moral decisions and judgements" (Gert, 2004: v). Clearly what follows is a Western view, though it is claimed to be based on universal features of "human nature such as our fallibility, rationality, and vulnerability" (Pritchard, 2006: 21). Gert

---

[10] The third aspect of virtue ethics, *endaimoni*, is achieved by knowing what things in life are more important than others; what is more relevant to the way one ought to live in the broadest sense. For example, living well is not merely to maximise physical pleasure or luxury. It is rather the satisfaction and contentment that is presumed to come from living a virtuous life. However for Aristotle there is no guarantee that virtue will yield well being. It also involves external things that are a matter of luck.

proposes 10 moral rules, which he regards as comprehensive. They are presented as the following two groups of 5:

1.   Do not kill

2.   Do not cause pain

3.   Do not disable

4.   Do not deprive of freedom

5.   Do not deprive of pleasure

6.   Do not deceive – virtue of truthfulness

7.   Keep your promises – virtue of dependability

8.   Do not cheat – virtue of fairness

9.   Obey the law – virtue of honesty

10. Do your duty –virtue of conscientiousness

The first 5 can be summarised as do not cause harm and the second 5 as do not violate trust. None of the rules are absolute, they are all contingent on circumstances, but according to Gert violations require a justification, therefore there are divergent answers to most controversial questions (2004: 38). The sense behind these 10 rules could be expressed differently. For example, Pritchard suggests a rule about fairness is absent, though it could be included under the rule about cheating. Sometimes fairness is taken as a synonym for morality itself. However unfairness can refer to something more specific, such as "punishing the innocent", or to not considering all readily available relevant facts when assessing someone's guilt or innocence, or to not hiring someone because she is not a white male, or to grading someone's paper without reading it carefully (or at all), and so on" (2006: 24). Children learn to make moral judgements and decisions by learning from adult instruction and by observing their example. Moral virtues develop from these experiences.

The first 5 rules do not have associated with them particular moral virtues, though violating them is associated with immorality. The second set of 5 have moral virtues associated with each of them as listed above. The virtues "all require knowing (but do not require being able to articulate) when it is justified to break the moral rule" (Gert, 2004: 77).

One may consider the ethics expressed in professional Ethical Codes, particularly those in the character/values category of types of obligations found in all these codes (see Section 2.4.1 below) as something like a "common morality". However we would argue that the character/values expected in professional codes are either more strict or more broadly defined, or there are more of them, than those expected of ordinary citizens according to the common morality. Arguably they are, taken as a whole, more like the virtues expected of nineteenth century *gentlemen*. Mason (1982: 12) points out, even going as far back as Chaucer, the concept of *gentillesse* was thought of as a constellation of moral qualities - such as generosity, openheartedness, magnanimity and courtesy to women - that ought go with gentle birth, but did not always do so.[11]

2.3 Defining professional ethics: codes of individual professions

In the second book in our series on professional ethics we distinguished three dimensions to Ethical Codes: types of obligations, to whom obligations are owed, what is the level of compulsion towards fulfilling the obligation as expressed in the language used in the code (Friedman et al., 2005). We contend that these are important ways of distinguishing what different professions regard as ethical competence, even if they do not use this particular term, or at least they indicate what certain leaders of the profession regarded as ethical competence to be at the time when the code was developed or revised. The extent to which the code represents an accurate reflection of how the main body of the profession regards ethical competence depends on many things, given that the codes do not arise automatically from the

---

[11] There are other aspects of the constellation of characteristics of the gentleman, which are not clearly related to the general conception of the professional. One traditional example is the connection between being a gentleman and courtly love, or the pursuit of an idealised woman. Another, which was embellished in Victorian times, was the connection between being a gentleman and being a sportsman (see Mason, 1982 for accounts of both of these aspects of being a gentleman).

association, but rather they reflect a process that has been executed by people. Considerations include:

- Who those people are? Are they representative only of a small subset of the profession, the leaders, those at the top of the profession, those who are older than most of the rest?

- When was the code produced or revised? Ethical competence can and does change in time, as evidenced by changes that are periodically made to codes.

- What was the process by which the code was produced, in particular, was the general membership consulted? Also were other association codes used as guides or templates? If so there may be a tendency for codes to resemble each other rather than reflecting the peculiarities of the particular profession concerned. However this influence may be countered if codes are developed or revised at a time when certain specific (and possibly time dependent) issues concerned the profession.

In spite of these complicating factors, we must accept that however the code was developed and whoever's vision of ethical competence it represents, the code is there as a focus for how the profession both educates its own and how it is viewed by the outside world. Whether the code is merely aspirational or the foundation for disciplinary action, it will, to a greater or lesser extent, become the distillation of ethical competence for members of the profession.

2.3.1   Types of obligations

Considering professional codes, Friedman et al. (2005) distinguish 4 types of obligations defined in many codes. These are:

1.   Good citizenship

2.   Character/values

3.   Expertise/competence

4.   Conduct re:

    o people

40

- o business

- o general

The first of these categories emphasises that professional associations expect their members to be good citizens as well as good or ethical professionals. This includes general obligations to obey the laws of the land or local social norms, or injunctions to obey certain specific laws, such as anti-discrimination laws.

The second category contains a wide range of obligations. Some obligations in this category would be expected of any good citizen; some are specific to professionals in general; some are specific to certain professions. Obligations expected of any good citizen would be honesty, integrity and courtesy, though it may be that professional associations (and society) expect a higher standard of honesty, integrity and courtesy of professionals than of other citizens, or a higher standard of individuals in their professional roles than when they act in other roles, such as in the family or meeting in public places.[12] For example, a degree of selflessness is required largely in relation to client interests, but also towards other members of the profession. For example "Members shall ensure, so far as they are able, that other engineers receive credit for their professional achievements and receive whatever rewards to which they are entitled" (The Institution of Engineers of Ireland).

Some obligations are common to most professions, but not necessarily an obligation expected of non-professionals, such as independence. Certain obligations would apply only to certain professions, such as confidentiality, which may be a feature only of professions where clients are particularly vulnerable. That is, it relates to structural and cultural situations that are specific to certain occupations. Mistakes or

---

[12] The degree to which there is a distinction between obligations of individuals in their formal professional roles and their obligations in other roles is likely to vary by profession. It certainly seems to have changed over time. In the past the distinction was less clear. For example, in Victorian times a gentleman was expected to behave in certain ways, whatever the circumstances (Mason, 1982). Nowadays this distinction can be more clearly drawn, particularly for less high-profile professions of today such as specialist managers within companies not offering that specialism as a professional service. On the other hand, for people in high profile professions associated with media interest, such as doctors and teachers, the tide seems to be moving in the other direction, with an acceptance that the public should be informed by the media when the personal behaviour of professionals falls below the standard expected of them in their role as professionals.

substandard work by some professionals are more likely to lead to harm (and even death) to members of the public who are not direct clients, such as engineers or construction professionals.

In addition there will be instances where some professions reflect changes in social norms more quickly or more fully than others. This will also be related to structural conditions particular to certain professions, such as for engineers. For example, the Engineers of Ireland have devoted a major section of their code to 'Environmental & Social Obligations'. Six clauses out of the 29, more than a fifth of the code, refer to the environment. These clauses involve not only that members "shall have due regard to the ... impacts [of their work] on the natural environment" and that the projects they work on shall "have minimal adverse effects on the environment", but also that members "shall promote the principles and practices of sustainable development and the needs of present and future generations" and that they should strive for the "most efficient consumption of natural resources which is practicable economically, including the maximum reduction in energy usage, waste and pollution". Even further, that members "shall foster environmental awareness within the profession and among the public" and even more specifically:

> *Members shall promote the importance of social and environmental factors to professional colleagues, employers and clients with whom they share responsibility and collaborate with other professions to mitigate the adverse impacts of their common endeavours.*

Here we clearly have obligations that are beyond what would be expected of the ordinary citizen. Many codes of conduct for other professions do not include any specific environmental obligations.[13]

The next category of obligations distinguished by Friedman et al., are more specifically related to professionals as experts. They also concern aspects of conduct that would not normally be expected, or at least not be so specifically expected, of non-professionals (or of professionals in other aspects of their lives). Non-professionals need not be particularly competent in what they do as an obligation. Those who are training to be professionals are not expected to be competent. Professionals are not expected (generally) to be competent at activities

---

[13] This does not preclude inclusion of such obligations in more professional codes in future.

42

unrelated to their professional occupation. Competence expectations are generally higher, or more strictly expected, of professionals than those in non-professional occupations.

The items typically included under expertise/competence are related to ethical competence in a somewhat different manner than those concerned with character or values. They are generally more specific. By far the most common was maintaining of one's own competence, which is connected to the growing importance of the obligation to carry out and keep up continuing professional development. For example,

> *In all circumstances members ... must seek continually to improve their performance and update and refresh their skills and knowledge.*
> (CIPD Chartered Institute of Personnel Development)

> *As a professional manager you will ... keep up-to-date with developments in best management practice and continue to develop personal competence.*
> (CMI Chartered Management Institute)

> *A member shall ... be encouraged to register for the Institute's scheme of Continuing Professional Development.*
> (CIM Chartered Institute of Marketing)

Here is where ethical competence and technical competence cross, in that, when statements such as these are included in professional Ethical Codes, they indicate an ethical obligation to keep up one's technical competence.

Exercising competence and working within competence were next in popularity. The latter is most clearly an obligation to ethical competence. For example,

> *In particular as a doctor you must ... recognise the limits of your professional competence.*
> (GMC General Medical Council)

> *Members must base all your actions and actions on these core values: ... Act within your limitations: be aware of the limits of your competence and don't be tempted to work beyond these. Never commit to more than you can deliver.*
> (RICS Royal Institute of Chartered Surveyors)

43

These statements refer to the aspect of ethical competence that we have labelled forbearance.

The types of obligations Friedman et al. label as conduct are common. A high proportion of statements in codes, particularly for public sector professionals, relate to obligations to behave in certain ways towards specific people. Items in this category include safeguarding others, minimizing the risks to which they are exposed. Also respecting the dignity and privacy of clients as well as their views. Another obligation in this category is to support the CPD of colleagues. Other obligations in this category concerned effective communication and consultation.

This brings us to the next subcategory under conduct; that is, conduct of business. Several concerned resources. For example

> *Members must be able to ... provide... the financial and technical resources appropriate for their work.*
> (RIBA Royal Institute of British Architects)

> *As regards the organization as a professional manager you will ... safeguard the assets ... of the organization. As regards the wider community as a professional manager you will ... seek to conserve resources wherever possible.*
> (CMI Chartered Management Institute)

The final subcategory, conduct in general had a disparate collection of items. These included upholding the reputation of the association and the profession, managing conflicts of interest, whistleblowing, competing fairly and matters relating to the code itself (that is, obligations to observe the code and keep up-to-date with changes in the code).

2.3.2   To whom obligations are owed

Generally the prime category of people to whom professional obligations are owed would be clients or patients. It is here that it we may consider professional ethics to be more clearly distinguishable from the ethical expectations of ordinary citizens. For example in market dealing, according to the law and social norms, *caveat emptor*, is a principle that non-professionals can fall back on. Clearly certain individuals in society would consider this to be too low a principle of

44

ethical obligation towards customers or clients, even for non-professionals. However for professionals the norm expected would be at a higher level. While ordinary people would be expected not to lie, they may not be expected to tell the whole truth. A car salesman would not be generally expected to point out all less obvious faults to potential customers, while a doctor would be expected to inform patients of negative side effects of treatments.

The range of beneficiaries of obligations beyond clients/patients in many codes is quite broad. In addition to obligations to the general public, obligations have been owed in the codes analysed in Friedman et al. (2005) to employers, the profession, the professional association, workplace subordinates, colleagues and the self. Unsurprisingly, business and management professions were more likely to have obligations owed to employers and workplace subordinates. Professions mostly in the public sector had a strong preponderance of obligations towards the client/patient, rather than the other beneficiaries.

2.3.3 Strength of compulsion or 'modality' of language of obligation

This third dimension of the codes is worth examining for two reasons. First, the language of the code can indicate how aspirational the code is. If the language is very strict, that is, if obligations are expressed as things one "must always" do or do "under any circumstances" or "shall do at all times" or "shall do in all respects", it is likely to be either highly aspirational or more likely it is a serious code that is used for semi-legal purposes as an anchor for disciplining members. Second, the language can distinguish the relative importance of different obligations and obligations to different stakeholders. Some obligations may be expressed as above, in very strict terms, while others may imply a lower level of compulsion, such as things that the professional "should" or "ought" to do; or even less strictly things that the professional should "seek to do" or do "when time permits", or should be "encouraged to" do. These are all phrases from codes analysed by Friedman et al. and in that book a hierarchy of levels of compulsion is presented (2005: 110).

- Chapter 3 -
Foundations: competencies, competence and performance; enabling capabilities, dispositions and motivations

3.1   Introduction

Competence is a very popular and a seemingly very positive word. However it has many shades of meaning and the term is often used in a misleading way. We therefore begin with a discussion of definitions. In Section 3.2 we distinguish definitions of competency, competencies and competences on one hand from competence on the other, and relate all these concepts to performance. We illustrate this with a model.

Acquiring competencies and achieving professional competence relies on certain individual capabilities and personal characteristics that are 'carried' by individuals into the period of initial professional education and training. These capabilities and characteristics are not fixed at any moment of time, and can be shaped and honed during professional practice. Nevertheless professional bodies do attempt to attract individuals who have already demonstrated these capabilities and characteristics. In Section 3.3 we examine these personal foundations for professional competencies and competence: capacity to learn and certain dispositions and motivations.

We conclude with a brief discussion of the relationship between professional competence and organisational competence. We also comment on the distinction between on the one hand, competencies, competence and performance, and on the other hand what we described as personal foundations.

3.2 Defining competence, competency, competencies and competences

The word *competent* comes from the Latin *competere* in the sense of to "be fit, proper, or qualified". It appears as meaning "legally qualified" or "sufficient" from the 15th Century and "properly qualified" in the 17th Century according to the Oxford English Dictionary (OED). *Competency* is defined as "a sufficiency, without superfluity, of the means of life; the condition of having sufficient income". These definitions are dated at the end of the 16th Century according to the OED. Interestingly the Shorter OED edition of 1973 does not contain the words competences or competencies. But the most recent edition of the dictionary (2002) does.

There are three sources of confusion concerning competency.

First, there is a distinction between the positive sense of the definition, "sufficiency" or "qualified" and the less positive sense of "without superfluity". This distinction has been emphasised by Eraut as follows: "Competence ... [can have] the positive meaning of "getting the job done" or the negative meaning of "adequate but less than excellent" (1994: 166).

This suggests that competence may be inadequate or perhaps outdated in the 'modern' business world, which has been influenced since the 1980s by the excellence movement. Companies that succeed stand out from the rest as "excellent", they exceed expectations (see the classic statement of business "excellence" by Peters and Waterman, 1982). However we note in Section 3.4 that there are other lines of management thought that celebrate competencies and competence as critical for organisation success.

A second complication of the term is that it can be confused with performance. That sense of sufficiency can lead to the implication that being qualified and performing sufficiently are synonymous. This issue is clarified by Pithers who states broadly that: "Competency is about what attributes underlie successful performance" (1998: 2), and more clearly by Messick who states:

> *Competence refers to what a person knows and can do under ideal circumstances, whereas performance refers to what is actually done under existing circumstances. Competence*

embraces the structure of knowledge and abilities, whereas performance subsumes as well the process of accessing and utilising those structures and a host of affective, motivational, attentional and stylistic factors that influence the ultimate responses. Thus, a student's competence might not be validly revealed in either classroom performance or test performance because of personal or circumstantial factors that affect behaviour.
(1984: 216-217)

This raises a *third* complication, the relation between competence and certain attributes such as positive attitudes towards work, skills and a person's knowledge base.

Eraut (1994: 179) points to a distinction in the American literature between:

competence – *"a person's overall capacity",* and
competency – *"specific capabilities".*

This is similar to Rylatt and Lohan, who define competencies as: "... a description of the essential skills, knowledge and attitudes required for effective performance in a work situation" (1995: 47).

This is approaching the way the term competency is being used more recently. For example competencies are defined by the Human Resource System Group as:

General descriptions of the behaviour or actions needed to successfully perform within a particular [work] context (e.g. job, group of jobs, function, etc). While competencies are not new, what is new is their increased application across human resource functions to drive both employee and corporate performance and realize results that are relevant to the organization's business strategies and vision.
(www.hrsg.ca)

Competencies or competences are increasingly used by human resource functions to drive performance. They are interpreted as building blocks for creating job descriptions in recruitment and for job evaluations, and to identify training needs and learning outcomes.

According to the Chartered Institute of Personnel Development (CIPD) website (www.cipd.co.uk):

> *Competency = "the behaviours that employees must have, or must acquire, to input into a situation in order to achieve high levels of performance"*
> *Competence = "a system of minimum standards or is demonstrated by performance and outputs. It implies an outcome-based approach to knowledge and learning."*

It is interesting to compare this CIPD definition and that of Rylatt and Lohan above. Together they imply a two-way relationship between competency/competence and performance. On one hand competencies are necessary conditions for effective performance in particular work situations. On the other hand effective performance demonstrates competence. This can then indicate the likelihood of future effective or successful performance.

Gonzi et al. (1993: 5-6) provide a somewhat different view of the relationship between competence and certain attributes such as knowledge and attitudes as well as performance. They say that:

> *The competence of professionals derives from their possessing a set of relevant attributes such as knowledge, skills and attitudes. These attributes which jointly underlie competence are often referred to as competencies. So a competency is a combination of attributes underlying some aspect of successful professional performance ... attributes of individuals do not in themselves constitute competence. Nor is competence the mere performance of a series of tasks. Rather, the notion of competence integrates attributes with performance.*

We may summarise what we regard to be a consistent and comprehensive view of the relationships described above (at least what appears to be the majority opinion) by the model shown in Figure 3:1.

Figure 3:1 Competency-performance-competence relations

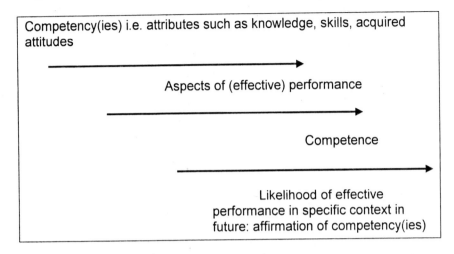

Note that we have qualified attitudes as acquired attitudes rather than leaving it as Gonzi has formulated competencies. This is because we want to distinguish attitudes acquired during the acquisition of competencies from attitudes and motivations that individuals bring to their pre-professional training or practicing situation. We distinguish between what CIPD call the behaviours individuals have, from those they must acquire. In this we distinguish capability from competence. We take the word capability to mean the constellation of knowledge, skills, attitudes and dispositions that people bring to the acquisition of competencies needed for professional practice. Capabilities generally refer to behaviours acquired in the home, at school, and among social contacts during early years. Some of these capabilities may also be genetic or part of our physiology, some are learned, and some may be learned very early in life. These issues are discussed more fully in Section 3.3.

3.2.1 Two views of competency-based education and training (CBE or CBT)

As indicated above, competency-competences-competencies are general terms used to indicate a range of attributes or the outcome of a range of attributes such as knowledge, skills and attitudes. They are terms used to indicate the attributes contributing to performance, while competence is a broader term. It indicates a state that a person reached that has been evidenced by performance as well as competencies. It is also regarded as an indicator, or even a guarantee, of performance above a certain standard in future situations. Competence is an indicator of likely sufficiency in future performance or actual practice.

Recently this constellation of terms has acquired more specific meanings associated with changes in thinking about education and training. This has been prompted by the perceived problem that education and training had become disconnected with what is increasingly regarded as the 'proper' outcome of this activity, that is, with work and the requirements of employers.[14] This has led to a further division of meanings for the term competency; that is, between a narrow and a broad view of it (Chappell *et al.*, 2000). The difference turns on the distinctions described above between attributes, competency, competence and performance.

Narrow views are based on the idea that: "...standardised training outcomes can be achieved by all learners if a thorough analysis of the behaviours demonstrated by any competent performer is undertaken and then transposed onto a set of standardised learning sequences" (Chappell *et al.*, 2000: 192).

This is based on the Taylorian view (Taylor, 1911) that most jobs require only clear and simple steps that can be learned by almost anyone with little prior knowledge, or that jobs can be designed to require a minimum degree of skill. Hackett points out "This narrow view of competence is often criticised as not taking adequate account of the social, intellectual, emotional and process facets of the various educational setting and circumstances in which CBT is practiced" (2001: 105).

For example, CBT is criticised for its tendency "... to overemphasise the routine, visible aspects of work and to neglect "under-the-surface" skills like problem solving and information handling" (Field, 2000: 168)

The broad view is more recent. According to Chappell *et al.* (2000) this broad view:

---

[14] We note that there is a view of education, particularly among some educationalists, that education should be an end in itself, that educational institutions should stimulate and guide individual thirst for knowledge and contribute to wisdom and the appreciation of life's rich possibilities; that is, to *endaimonia* as described in Chapter 2.

... does not confuse performance with competence, and argues that a large variety of attributes that underpin performance must be considered in any competence analysis. It rejects single acceptable outcomes as being indicative of competent performance, proposing that in most situations multivariable contexts inevitably lead to multivariable outcomes. ... it emphasises human agency and social interrelations in competency descriptions. It regards competence as developmental and elaborative rather than static and minimalist.
(2000: 196-197)

Here we take this broad view of competence, but consider the narrow view as more relevant for competencies. Competency-based education or training can be narrow if it is limited to individual competencies and if those competencies are considered in isolation from each other. Broad competency-based education and training regards individual competencies as leading to competence, but only if individuals have a *range* of these narrow competencies in their repertoire. This leads to a critical distinction of the broad approach; that is, that competence requires an understanding of both the wider likely consequences of exercising individual competencies and an understanding of what alternatives can be pursued which may involve recommending actions or carrying out actions that are not part of the knowledge, skills and behaviours that are included in what would be taught as the narrow competency. It requires a *critical* understanding of competencies and an appreciation of when those competencies should not be exercised, and what alternatives could be invoked.

The broad view of competence is in keeping with the philosophy behind those who initiated the CPD movement: that professionals need to develop their professional competence throughout their lives and that this involves more than accumulating knowledge of techniques.

The first official definition of the term Continuing Professional Development was developed in the UK by the CPD in Construction Group in 1986.

The systematic maintenance, improvement and broadening of knowledge, skills and development of personal qualities necessary for the execution of professional and technical duties throughout the practitioner's working life.

This has been the most widely adopted and quoted definition of CPD (Friedman et al, 2000). According to it CPD involves the accumulation of competencies, but not as isolated knowledge, skills and attitudes or personal qualities. Rather they are contributions to a repertoire of competencies that together represent professional competence.

Cheetham and Chivers (2005) argue that many models of competence are limited to *functional* competence models. They define functional competence as "the ability to perform a range of work-based tasks effectively to produce required outcomes" (2005: 87). We identify this as the narrow approach to competence and prefer the label competency. They also note that these approaches tend to be used more for assessment, for qualifications purposes, rather than development. Overall Marshall (1991: 63) argues that the functional competencies associated with the NVQ (National Vocational Qualification) model "becomes less effective as the level of skill and cognitive requirement increases." Cheetham and Chivers criticise approaches that focus only on functional competency for their limited understanding of knowledge and personal/behavioural competencies, and the difficulty of accommodating an ethical dimension.

We agree wholeheartedly with Cheetham and Chivers on the inadequacy of functional competency approaches to capture professional competence. We have argued that this is a danger in applying the government's skills and competency agenda to the professions, an approach designed originally to deal with 16 to 19-year old school leavers who are not expected to go on to higher or further education (see Friedman, 2005).

Criticism of the narrow view may be interpreted as inability or unwillingness to recognise that the items in Figure 3:1 are distinct. There are processes or steps that must be taken or stages that must be reached to move from competencies to performance and from competencies and performance experiences to competence. Another and related way to view the distinction is that the narrow view undervalues the repertoire of related knowledge, skills and attributes that are required for successful performance and that arise from the achievement of competence. It is possible in a constrained situation to achieve competency in a particular task without some broader achievement of competence. However, the danger of this is that when situations arise that are regarded as exceptional, the narrowly defined competency will not be sufficient. We may then consider a range of activities that run from those where narrow competency is likely to be sufficient for almost all situations, to ones where the variation of situations and uncertainty about how those variations will occur, make a narrow view of competency virtually useless. Those activities and occupations are the ones described as likely to be professionalized in Chapter 1 (Section 1.2).

3.3 Foundations for competencies and competence: learning capacity, dispositions and motivations

There is an approach to competence, particularly associated with professionals, and among them, particularly applying to managers, which emphasises personal characteristics. The leading example of this approach is Boyatzis (1982). Cheetham and Chivers label this as the personal competence approach, which they define as "the ability to adopt appropriate observable behaviours in work related situations" (2005: 88). This approach has been commonly used in order to assess recruits and promotion potential in managers (Woodruffe, 1990; Dale and Iles, 1992; McGaghie, 1993).

We regard personal competence, which Boyatzis identifies with professional competence and Cheetham and Chivers regard as a component of the core of professional competence, in a different light, as a *foundation* for professional competence, rather than the 'real thing'.

For the kind of activities that professionals undertake, it is important that they have a wider repertoire of behavioural patterns than are required for a standard execution of a task. Professional work is characterised by considerable discretion and autonomy, which are required to decide not only how to perform a service, but also to decide which of several services (or nuances of services or aspects of services) are appropriate to the particular situation at hand.

We distinguish two different types of personal characteristics that are foundations for professional ethical competence (and professional technical competence). These are learning capacity and motivation or disposition.

3.3.1 Learning capability

Competence requires a base of individual capability to master particular techniques. This is largely established for individuals by the time they come to occupational training. However it is also a factor during that training. The matching of abilities to the task of acquiring certain techniques rather than others has occupied education theorists for some time (Kolb, 1984). Opinions are divided about the extent to which attributes such as ability to memorise things, potential manual dexterity and mental agility contribute to the ability both to acquire competencies and to apply them to specific circumstances. There is also debate as to the extent to which these attributes are genetic, or acquired early in life or can be developed throughout ones lifetime. Various screening processes are designed to filter for these attributes at various points in educational development and professional qualifications. There is always a debate about how effective these screening techniques are because at any point in one's educational development other factors can come into play to enhance or detract from one's performance at these tests. In particular the next foundation factor, motivation, is an important source of variation in performance at tests and a complicating factor in the use of test results to predict likelihood of success in future acquisition of competency. It is also very difficult, if not impossible, to remove social and cultural biases in these tests. Such biases may reflect biases in client expectations for professional practitioners, and so may not be so great a problem if the ability to meet client expectations is what is being tested for. However client biases change over time. In the time between an individual taking such tests in early life, and coming to practice, some of these biases may be reduced or removed, or altered.

3.3.2 Dispositions and motivations

Often these characteristics are tested in aptitude tests. They relate both to particular collections of dispositions, such as the disposition to work more with people or with numbers; to work more with theoretical concepts or practical manual problems. They also relate to 'character' in the overall sense of those characteristics that are considered broadly to be of value for professionalism, whatever particular practice is involved as well as certain character traits that may be more prized in certain professions than others (attention to detail, creativity, willingness to take responsibility, leadership qualities). The components of character can sometimes be those specified in the values professionals are expected to demonstrate as in professional Ethical Codes: notably honesty, integrity, fairness and reliability (see Chapter 2 and Friedman et al. 2005). The manner in which characteristics or dispositions and overall character affects performance will also depend on (or be mediated by) context-specific factors; such as mood and perception of interests, links to ideas, and sympathy with culture. These things are more ephemeral. Some people are more inclined to be swayed by current mood and sympathies than others. Finally there are the more proximate factors underlying motivation both to acquire competencies and to achieve effective performance. Money, status, a sense of calling, the desire to be associated with a certain group of people; can all affect individual motivation. Some minimum combination of these motivating factors will be necessary to achieve competency and competence.

3.3.3 Sources of disposition and capability

Dispositions towards learning and towards certain ethical behaviours that are expected of professionals can be developed within the environments of family, schooling and other social connections. Perhaps a distinction these days is that it is accepted by most that school leavers have only rudimentary technical competence and require further training of some sort in order to get reasonable jobs or to enter a profession. It is not so well accepted that school leavers have only a rudimentary ethical competence in the sense of whatever level of *ethical* competence may be required of them to perform good work. In the past good breeding, perhaps supported by attending the right sort of school, was assumed to lead to an appropriate sense of ethical competence. In Victorian times and earlier, having come from a 'good' family meant that one was a gentleman and Ethical Codes of the professions obliged gentlemanly behaviour. Traces of this view may be seen in Ethical Codes today, but obligations towards gentlemanly behaviour have been either toned down or augmented with other obligations, particularly ones that are more closely related to competence. In fact before the mid-19th Century few professions had formal Ethical Codes. It was assumed that all members of the profession were gentlemen and that they all knew what obligations were expected of gentlemen.

3.4   Conclusions

In Section 3.2 we noted that competence, meaning adequate but less than excellent, may be an outdated concept in view of the 'excellence' movement in management thought. However there is a different line of management thought that emphasises the critical importance of competencies and competence, and in particular the concept of 'core' competencies and particularly 'core' competence of organisations. One interesting distinction between the 1973 and 2002 versions of the Shorter Oxford English Dictionary is that competency in the more recent version of the dictionary also includes the meaning of rivalry and competition. This reflects an important current of management thought which has developed since the 1970s. According to Schmiedinger et al. (2005: 162)

> *In the era of the knowledge based society the objective orientated utilization and development of organizational competencies become the major driving force for organizational success. In order to stay competitive organizations of all industries and sizes have to make use of their consciously used and in many cases 'hidden' knowledge related organizational competencies.*

The term "core competencies" now has wide currency in the management literature. According to the primary expression of this view, a company's competitiveness derives from its core competencies (Prahalad and Hamel, 1990). "Core competencies are the collective learning in the organization, especially the capacity to coordinate diverse production skills and integrate multiple streams of technologies" (1990: 82).

A critical distinction between professional competencies and professional competence on one hand and the notion of core organisation competencies on the other is in the manner in which management theorists have conceived of how core competencies arise.

First, they may be consciously acquired or developed. That is, either consciously picked up in the recruitment of individuals with particular competencies and the purchase of other resources (this can include the purchase of whole companies as well as taking on certain facilities) or consciously developed in house through company training (both formal off site and more informal on the job training). Prahalad and

Hamel emphasise how Japanese companies in the 1980s acquired core competencies through partnerships with other companies.

Second, they may be acquired unwittingly, locked in the tacit or hidden knowledge that either accompanies individuals hired (items that might be included in a CV for a different job than the one the person was hired for) or generated within a company as a result of organisational activities, but which occur incidentally to that activity. For example people develop in house jargon to communicate more efficiently, but do not acknowledge this jargon as an organisation resource. According to Prahalad and Hamel the whole concept of a corporation needs to be rethought as a set of core competencies rather than a set of business units or an offering of particular end products. It is easy to miss what those competencies are if you are only looking at the products and the accounting entities which are most visible aspects of the corporation to the outsider, and which may monopolise the attention of management.

In the management literature, for private companies, both conscious and hidden resources available to organisations as their core competencies, develop in response to market forces and the particular strategies to deal with market opportunities and threats generated mainly by top management. They are what is required to meet long term corporate goals, to develop the products and services of the future. The way competencies are defined depends critically on what employing organisations consider to be the packages of technical abilities relevant to meeting current and future market forces. Competencies that are developed according to this notion of core competencies generally exclude the role of professional bodies and miss out the importance of professional competence. However, particularly for professional services firms, but also for any organisation that employs a significant proportion of professionals, an important competitive aim must be to develop confidence and trust in the quality of professional services offered or used in the development of products or other services. This can be just as important as technical competencies. For professional services firms we would consider the ethical competence of their employees and partners to be a major component of their core competence.

In the next chapter we connect the discussion of professional ethics provided in Chapter 2 with the discussion of competence, capability and performance of this chapter in order to distinguish professional ethical competence from other forms of competencies and competence as well as from professional technical competence.

- Chapter 4 -
Stages to ethical competence

4.1 Introduction

In Chapter 2 we explored professional ethics. In Chapter 3 we defined and explored competence and the relation between competencies and competence as well as their foundations: capability and disposition or motivation. In Section 4.2 we combine those ideas to present an understanding of ethical competence in terms of a series of stages. We then in Section 4.3 concentrate on distinguishing the final stage, ethical competence, from the stage before it, technical competence. We propose that ethical competence is the hallmark of professionalism and should be more commonly and deeply appreciated as such. There is another broad concept that is often considered to be the hallmark of professional practice; reflective practice. In Section 4.4 we provide some background to this concept and then relate it to ethical competence. Finally in Section 4.5 we examine ethical competence from the point of view of phases in the execution of ethical competence rather than how it is acquired.

4.2 Stages in the acquisition of ethical competence

What is instilled as part of professional training and membership of a professional community of practice, overseen by a professional association, can be thought of as being acquired through five steps or stages.

1. Personal capability, disposition and motivation

2. Knowledge acquisition

3. Competencies

4. Technical competence

5. Ethical competence

The order of these stages need not be followed in strict sequence in time from stage 1 through to 5. Rather the stages represent a logical series that we believe will usually be achieved in the sequence presented here. In particular ethical competence is presented here as a step or stage beyond technical competence.

Figure 4:1 Stages towards ethical competence

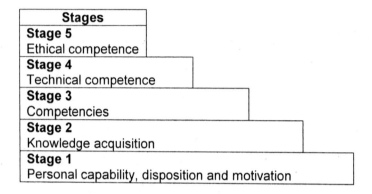

Stages
Stage 5 Ethical competence
Stage 4 Technical competence
Stage 3 Competencies
Stage 2 Knowledge acquisition
Stage 1 Personal capability, disposition and motivation

4.2.1   Personal characteristics: learning capability, disposition and motivation

These have been described in the previous chapter. Together these elements may be regarded as foundations for both technical and ethical competence: the learning capability more for technical competence, and the disposition and motivation aspects perhaps more for ethical competence. The latter comprise what may be thought of as what is embraced by the term 'character'.

4.2.2   Knowledge acquisition: theoretical and generic knowledge, as well as knowledge of techniques

Knowledge is more than information or pure data. It is information in a context of some sort of systematic basis. Initial professional qualifications will, for traditional occupations, involve a university degree or postgraduate qualification. However, some of the newer occupations that have become professionalised or are becoming professionalised require other types of educational qualifications. This may be gained through standard formal education, but it can also be gained through informal means; reading books and articles, finding things on the Internet, listening to others, watching others, reflecting on experiences. Most traditional professions have their origins in craft occupations, which were accessed through apprenticeship. Traditional professions such as law and medicine still have essential apprenticeship components, but only after formal higher education. The pure experience route, particularly as monitored by established practitioners, is common in some occupations at early stages of professionalisation today.

We distinguish three aspects of the knowledge base that are necessary as part of the stage of knowledge acquisition.

First is what is learned while acquiring formal initial professional qualifications: the theoretical basis of the field of practice. This is typically acquired on higher and further education courses that cover a general subject, such as in a physics or economics degree. Much of this theory in not directly applicable to eventual professional practice and appears to be more important for those who will eventually become academics.

A second aspect of knowledge acquisition concerns what are known as generic, transferable or key skills.[15] The National Advisory Board for Public Sector Higher Education and the University Grants Committee (NAB/UGC, 1984: 4) issued an early statement on generic skills that could be delivered by higher education in order to link with employer requirements. They identified abilities to:

- Analyse complex issues

- Identify the core of a problem and the means of solving it

- Synthesise and integrate disparate elements

- Clarify values

- Make effective use of numerical and other information

- Work co-operatively and constructively with others

- Communicate clearly both orally and in writing.

---

[15] Between the mid 1980s and mid 1990s the more common term used was *transferable* skills (NAB/UGC, 1984; Smith et al., 1989; Allen, 1993). Key skills became more popular after it was recommending by the Dearing report (Dearing, 1996).

The Board proposed these in recognition of how rapidly specific technical knowledge can become outdated in the modern world. These skills were not intended to replace such technical knowledge, but rather they would contribute to the knowledge base that would be valued by private and public sector employers, regardless of particular profession. Since then many parallel lists of 'transferable' skills have been developed, one with a list of over 100 (Allen, 1993), and causing some confusion (Murphy and Otter 1999). Again, acquiring these skills is not the same as acquiring the capacity to apply specific knowledge elements in practice circumstances. Rather these are the sorts of things that can be taught in non-practice situations that are closer to the capacities that must be linked to knowledge in order to increase the likelihood that practitioners will be able to apply specific knowledge in real life practice situations. They are generic tools that can help in specific situations to translate specific competencies into more general competence.

For eventual practice a third element is critical, that is, acquiring understanding of certain specific techniques that are used in the field of practice. Techniques may be defined as ways of doing things. We would further distinguish them as ways of doing things that can be communicated to others. Some skills are implicit, hard to define formally, but they can still be communicated by demonstration.[16] Techniques may be considered in terms of a hierarchy of difficulty of mastering them. This may be defined fairly clearly in terms of how long it takes to master them, however there will always be a complicating factor in terms of how much manual dexterity is involved and how much conceptual understanding is needed. It may take different lengths of time to master these different things. Obviously there will also be differences in how long different individuals take to master particular techniques, which relates to foundation factors 3 and 4 described below. Techniques vary enormously in terms of what is required to acquire or to have mastered them.

1.   Some techniques may be imparted through instructions, much like the instructions provided in DIY assembly packs for furniture. The generalist background required to receive these techniques and to master them are presumed to be available to

---

[16] Technology may be defined as constellations of techniques that are focused around a material (such as plastics technology) or a piece of equipment (computer technology) or a particular activity (communication technology or transportation technology) or a knowledge field defined in the academy (biological technology, civil engineering technology), (see Friedman, 1994).

all with an expected minimum standard of ability and education background before they come to specific occupational training: ability to read, ability to handle relatively simple tools. 'Higher level' competencies, such as those that would allow one to be considered an expert in a field, are unlikely to be entirely of this type. Nevertheless with the Internet and the spread of distance learning, more and more higher-level skills are being imparted in packaged forms, without the benefit of face-to-face instruction.

2. Some techniques cannot be easily imparted by impersonal instructions and require the presence of a demonstrator, or instructor. They may require repeated demonstration and practice with the instructor pointing out adjustments needed by the acolyte in order to achieve the required technique. On the other hand they may require explanation and learners may need the opportunity to have their questions answered, though the latter can be achieved without the direct presence of an instructor. One measure of the quality of distance learning materials is the degree of interactivity these materials incorporate or allow.

3. Some techniques cannot be acquired in a short period because the required standard of competency involves a manual dexterity or a mental agility that cannot be achieved without considerable practice. Playing a musical instrument is a common example of this type.

4. Some techniques cannot be acquired without a deeper understanding of the theory by which the technique has been delivered and the context of the technique. When should the technique be applied and when not, under what circumstances will the technique be effective, and particularly, why. This then allows the future practitioner to judge when to use the technique and when not without complete elaboration of all the possibilities during training. Much of this knowledge may be imparted without practicing the technique.

4.2.3   Competency and competencies: ability to apply specific knowledge elements in practice circumstances

This can be acquired at the same time as knowledge and through the same processes. However, particularly in our formal education systems, there is a separation between knowledge acquisition and acquisition of the ability to apply that knowledge in 'real-life' situations. These competencies are defined outside the individual practitioner and outside formal education institutions and training bodies. They come from a number of sources.

a) The aims of employer organisations in the context of the demands of the user of the services and products provided by those organisations (possibly as interpreted by and mediated by government agencies or private training agencies).

Competencies are currently primarily associated with the skill requirements of employer organisations, or at least that is how the current government views it. Employers have increasingly realised that many fresh recruits do not have the appropriate competencies when they emerge from general education and for some, even after they have achieved formal professional qualifications. It is a challenge for awarding and accrediting bodies continually to redesign the curricula to reflect the changing requirements of employers, due to technological change and changes in management thinking. In this employer requirements will change in response to market forces, both in terms of where in the market organisations position themselves, and in terms of what techniques are developed by competitors.

This is the primary thrust of the current government's skills and competency agenda. The Sector Skills Councils and the Sector Skills Development Agency are intended to act as intermediaries between the employer-defined skills and competency requirements and suppliers of those skills and competencies. Originally professional bodies were almost completely ignored in spite of being long-standing players in that intermediary role between potential recruits to the professions and organised practice of the profession. This situation has changed somewhat, sometimes existing professional bodies are involved in the Sector Skills Councils (such as the involvement of the HCIMA and the IMI in their relevant Sector Skills Councils), often they are not.

For sole traders and individual practices the development of competencies may be still determined by the individual producer. The individual producer or practitioner decides what the market requires. Crafts people who set up to produce a product must be sensitive to market demand, but they determine the techniques they use. For professionals directly offering their services to clients, the market will also have an effect on the nature of the competencies required of them, and they will be affected more directly by these market pressures than if they were providing professional services to larger employers, particularly if those employers are providing goods and services to different markets.

A critical distinction that we make is that the clients or the markets are only shaping factors for affecting the techniques employers or sole traders require of their employees or of themselves.

b)   The manner in which the profession articulates its jurisdiction according to the knowledge base and according to client need (and/or the aims of the client).

Competence for professionals contains an extra element. This is the manner in which the subject base is formulated through the accreditation of professional bodies. This has two components. First is the problem basis from which clients come to professionals, and the way clients express their desires to professionals, that is, the demand side of the market and what lies behind the specific service demand. Second there is the manner in which possible knowledge is formulated into standards by a professional body, in itself affected by peers in practice and in academe. This leads to some aspects of the historical knowledge base being discarded or altered as new techniques are developed. This is a counterpart of the aims of the organisation in the context of which competency will be exercised, which will also depend on how demand for their products and services is expressed and how they interpret those demands in relation to the techniques available.

For professionals working as employees in non-specialised professional services organisations, there can be a conflict between the two foundations to their competence: organisational and professional.

We distinguish this stage of acquiring competencies from the previous stage, knowledge and technique acquisition, by the presumption that for knowledge acquired in educational and training institutions to become genuine competencies, they must be applied to practice situations. There are elements to any competency that require practice elements that can only be guessed at in education and training institutions. Facility with jargon used in particular situations by other practitioners; knowledge of what is expected by clients; operation of customised computer systems; understanding what is expected in billing when there are uncertainties; general understanding of the contextual features that render theoretical knowledge unexpectedly inappropriate in particular circumstances; all these can only be acquired in practice situations.

4.2.4 Technical competence

Technical competence may be defined as the ability to know when and how to draw on parts of one's knowledge repertoire and when to forbear from application on technical criteria (what will 'work' and what will not 'work'). Competency requires some degree of reflective practice, but this can be quite low, competence requires a much higher degree of reflective practice as we will discuss in Section 4.4 below. As noted in Chapter 3, technical competence requires foundations involving both the acquisition of competencies and the exercise of these competencies in effective performance. These in turn are based on individual capabilities and motivation or attitudes. A further factor considered in the previous stage is the added concrete specifications of competencies defined by and required by organisations or by professional bodies.

4.2.5 Ethical competence

Ethical competence for professionals may be defined as the ability to apply knowledge in an ethical manner as defined by Ethical Codes promulgated through professional associations, but not limited to these codes in detail. Ethical competence involves a range of obligations and beneficiaries of obligations that will differ for different professions. In general it will involve on one hand, a set of 'competencies' that can be taught, such as understanding the particular Ethical Code of the relevant profession; knowing when to apply and when to forbear from applying knowledge, based on ethical principles; being aware of other ethical concerns of professionals with whom one may work. On the other hand it will also involve what distinguishes ethical competency from ethical competence, knowing what is 'right' and not 'right' in the heat of particular practice situations, and acting in the 'right' way, taking into account client/patient needs as well as what is morally correct and sensitive to other stakeholders or expected beneficiaries. There are many elements to ethical competence. It will involve not claiming that procedures recommended are more effective than professionals truly believe them to be, pointing out risks involved in pursuing whatever procedures are recommended. This too requires reflection both on and in practice and needs to be supported by experience, preferably with obliging peers. It also requires balancing client wants with client needs or enlightened interests of the client. Should they have a procedure done to them to the hilt or hold back, should they have the more expensive procedures or at least be informed of both unwanted side effects and of cheaper alternatives? Also how much should the professional presume to know that is in their clients' true interests, if they are not those explicitly revealed by the client? Professional political analysts and economists have got themselves into trouble by assuming they know best what is in the interests of their clients. Similarly balancing client interests with those of other obligatees such as interests of the general public, but also colleagues, employers, subordinates, the profession and the self are ethical accomplishments or competencies that go into making an individual ethically competent.

Some professionals (typically lawyers and engineers, but often accountants and architects) are often finding themselves tasked with advising clients on what they can do to the limit of the law, or to the limit of acceptable risk, or the limit of physical mechanical tolerances. This is an aspect of exercising expertise. However these professionals should also consider the 'enlightened' or long run interests of such clients. They need to take into account long-term reputation risks, not only to themselves, but also to their clients and other possible stakeholders. This is a stage beyond guarding against conflicts of interest, which is usually taken to mean conflicts of interest between the professional themselves and their clients due to other obligations or other interests of the professional. Rather it is a need to take into account the conflicting pressures and interests of the client and other stakeholders. We note that sometimes this is even beyond what is explicitly noted in professional codes, though we believe it should be made explicit in them.

4.2.6   Sequencing of the stages

The stages are not offered as a strict sequence of acquisition in time. They are offered in the order shown above in part because we wish to highlight the importance of ethical competence as something more than technical competence and as something often left out or unacknowledged in certain formulations of educational policy, particularly in the UK since the 1980s.

Figure 4:2 Elaborating the stages to ethical competence

What is added	Stage
Experience with ethical dilemmas, recognising an ethical situation, knowing what is right, ethical reflective practice	**Stage 5** Ethical competence
Experience with several competencies, tacit knowing what works, technical reflective practice	**Stage 4** Technical competence
Apply specific knowledge and techniques in practice as defined by profession or employer, could include ethical competency	**Stage 3** Competencies
Theoretical and technical basis of the profession	**Stage 2** Knowledge acquisition
Learning & moral judgement capabilities, disposition & motivation to succeed at chosen profession	**Stage 1** Personal capability, disposition and motivation

It is possible to begin to develop an ethical perspective on knowledge at an early stage and arguably this is an essential part of acquiring initial professional qualifications. Similarly the capacity to apply knowledge can be developed before much knowledge is acquired as in apprenticeship situations. The latter two stages rely more on the experience of practice. However it is possible to develop an ethical sense or an understanding or instinct for what is right and wrong for professional conduct without any professional knowledge or experience (or at least with no formal training or working in a professional context. Three sources considered here are also of course key influences affecting capability and motivation to acquire technical competencies as well as ethical competencies (as noted in Chapter 3).

- *Family.* All family situations convey norms to children. Many family situations involve parents and other close relatives who are working professionals. Values, virtues and character traits associated with the professions can be conveyed by observation and experiences on the receiving end of being 'treated' as the children of professionals. It is likely that some of the way professionals feel obligated to clients or patients and other stakeholders will be copied in their relations with their children, nieces and nephews and cousins.

- *Contemporaries.* Friends who may be similarly socialised into professional values at home can be important. Professional values are likely to be reinforced by people living in 'professional neighbourhoods'.

- *School.* Here the influence of contemporaries will be widened and may be either concentrated or diluted depending on the mix of the school. The extra factor at school is the role of teachers. They, as professionals, can convey to their pupils professional values as well as specific knowledge, even if the subject is not citizenship or values. Pupils will experience how certain professionals deal with clients.

There is likely to be a strong relationship between all three elements: family, friends and schooling. This may lead to strong pre-professional training, inculcation of professional values among children with professional family backgrounds. The implication of these factors, which predate specific professional training and support for ethical competence, is that a substantial proportion of individuals will be sensitised to professional ethics at the time of entry into initial professional training, before they acquire specific professional knowledge or experience. If during professional training there is little or no specific training on ethical competence, then it is likely that there will be a strong differential among students as to who develops a strong feeling for ethical competence and who does not. Those already sensitised to these issues are likely to be thinking about the knowledge and experience they gain during initial training through a lens of relating back what they learn to how this training will place them into situations that require ethical competence.

However it is quite possible that some of the values and attitudes developed by observing practicing professionals will not represent the standards espoused by professional bodies in their Ethical Codes and codes of conduct. It would be naïve to think that professionals always demonstrate ethical competence and it may be that in their family and friendship relations professionals do not come up to the standards expected of them when they are dealing with clients or with other professionals, employers and workplace subordinates. Those who maintain the highest professional standards when dealing with people from behind the supports of their professional surroundings and their own mask of professional detachment, can behave in a much less professional manner when their personal emotions and expectations are concerned as for dealing with their own children. The home can be the place that professionals need in order to live for a time without some of the special obligations expected of a professional. Also what is expected of professionals changes over time, professional ethical and technical competence changes. For example, 30 years ago formal CPD was not expected of professionals and even today there is reluctance to follow CPD procedures, particularly on the part of older professionals. It may be that older professionals with whom young people are associated express and demonstrate older ethical values and attitudes, which are not compatible with current versions of professional ethical competence.

In these circumstances it may be that some will enter into professional training with a misconception of what ethical competence is and with certain attitudes and habits which are incompatible with ethical competence, such as the habit of not telling the truth and of disrespect.

The set of stages requires sufficient institutions for training and retraining potential and existing members with knowledge required to offer the services under the umbrella of their particular profession. Policies and programmes for initial qualifications, and recently also for CPD (Friedman et al 2000), need to be put in place and monitored by some agency, usually the professional association (though for initial qualifications this is usually in partnership with universities and colleges). Sometimes this involves on the job training leading to exams such as articling in law, residency in medicine and placements in accounting. In this time and as part of the full time formal knowledge acquisition, ethical aspects of the professional practice should be instilled. This is done by promulgating Ethical Codes, formal training in ethics of professional practice, usually through use of case studies of ethical dilemmas experienced by practitioners, and ultimately through making members of the profession aware of complaints and disciplinary procedures administered by the professional association or other regulatory body.

Finally ethical competence as the fifth stage may be thought of as both a limitation on competence and an enhancement of it. It is a limitation in that it provides reasons why unbridled technical competence can be harmful: that forbearance is necessary at certain times. However, this forbearance is in itself an enhancement in that if technical competence is exercised judiciously, it can be more successful, perhaps not in the short run, but in the long run and in terms of sustainability of both the individual expert and the practice of that specialist field.

The ethical competence path can be regarded not only as a way of maintaining a high quality of service, but also as a way to achieve consumer benefit, particularly consumer protection, which is not based on market competition (see Friedman, 2006).

4.3 Ethical competence vs technical competence

Aristotle begins book II of *Nichomanchean Ethics* by claiming that virtue is "of two kinds, intellectual and moral". Intellectual virtue begins and grows with teaching, but moral virtue comes as a result of habit. For the professional, we see a more intimate connection between ethical competence and technical competence. We see ethical competence as building on technical competence and also that certain forms of ethical competence are technical in themselves.

It is common for professional Ethical Codes to specify that it is an ethical obligation of members to *exercise* competence. This is interpreted here as technical competence, as it is distinguished from statements about values or character. Two other types of statements about professionals' obligations concerning their own competence are also distinguishable in codes; they are, to *maintain* professionals' own competence, and to work *within the limits* of their competence (see Friedman et al. 2005: 98-99). Sometimes statements about maintaining competence are written in general terms, such as to "keep up-to-date" or to "refresh skills", while others specifically mention the obligation to register for the association's CPD scheme. Statements to act only within the limits of one's competence were specifically mentioned in the General Medical Council code (2005: 63-64).

However there is a clear difference between ethical and technical competence, even for professionals. Carr (2005) drew a distinction that is close to that between ethical and technical competence.

In short, without denying any role or place for management or technique, the sharp end of the present claim is that good teaching is at heart more a matter of positive non-management and non-technical human (virtue ethical) association than of any more technically defined skills or competencies.
(2005: 270-271)

Carr was arguing against certain educational policies that have beleaguered teachers in the United Kingdom. That is, the emphasis on teachers providing evidence that would allow league tables for schools to be created and that would satisfy increasingly formal evidence requiring school inspectors. However Carr admits that both are relevant. He would perhaps disagree that technical competence is always a necessary stage to ethical competence. There is a dilemma here in his interpretation. On one hand he admits that part of being a good teacher is to have something to teach, to know one's subject. On the other hand he suggests that a good parent or friend may be more effective than a professional teacher in a school.

4.4 Ethical competence and reflective practice

Reflective practice is often viewed as the hallmark of professionalism. Here we make a case for ethical competence being the hallmark of professionalism or at least a combination of the two concepts. Technical Competence and Ethical Competence are not the same things as reflective practice, but they may be enhanced by it. To understand the relation between ethical competence and reflective practice we need to look behind the notion of reflective practice to views of reflectivity. Then we will deal more directly with conceptions of reflective practice, emphasising Schön's (1983) landmark contribution.

4.4.1 Reflectivity

According to Mezirow (1981) seven levels of reflectivity contribute to transformation (see O'Connor and Hyde (2005: 291-292). These are from the bottom to the top of the hierarchy:

a) The act of *reflectivity* – "awareness of a particular perception, meaning or behaviour relating to the self or of a habit in relation to seeing/thinking/acting"

b)   *Affective reflectivity* – awareness of one's feelings concerning how one perceives or acts or thinks

c)   *Discriminant reflectivity* – "assessing the efficacy of one's perceptions/thoughts/actions and habits of doing things; recognising reality contexts of situations and identifying immediate causes and relationships within situations"

d)   *Judgemental reflectivity* – "making and becoming aware of value judgements relating to perceptions, thoughts, actions and habits"

e)   *Conceptual reflectivity* – "critiquing one's own awareness having become aware of something, such as questioning the concepts one uses to evaluate another person"

f)   *Psychic reflectivity* – "recognising in oneself the habit of making premature judgements about others based on limited information, as well as recognising the interests and anticipations which influence the way one perceives/thinks/acts"

g)   *Theoretical reflectivity* – "awareness that a set of taken-for-granted cultural or psychological assumptions is responsible for the habit of making premature judgements and conceptual inadequacy."

We believe these can be simplified as comprising four aspects of reflectivity.

- General awareness of oneself as a perceiving, thinking and acting individual.

- Awareness of specific aspects of oneself in this context. Awareness of one's feelings and one's morality or value judgements, as a perceiving, thinking and acting individual.

- Assessment of how well one is doing with one's perceptions, thoughts and actions. This may involve awareness of the context and causes of the situation in which one perceives, thinks and acts.

- Taking of a critical approach to the three previous aspects of reflectivity. Awareness of the efficiency of one's actions by recognising habitual patterns and taken-for granted ways of seeing, thinking and acting, but also to take into account where these taken for granted ways come from, that is, what is the context in terms of culture and personal history or disposition or lack of conceptual tools.

We summarise all these aspects of reflectivity in Table 4:1. There are three levels of reflectivity: awareness, assessment and critique. Within each of these we distinguish two dimensions general vs specific and surface vs deep.

We may think of reflectivity, at its most primitive level, as involving only general awareness of one's being, as a perceiving, thinking and/or acting individual. This can still be classified in terms of general or specific and immediate or distant causality, but it may be that the distinction is only relevant at the two higher levels of assessment and critique.

At the level of assessment, specific techniques or ways of assessing one's perceptions, thoughts and actions can be discerned such as the manner in which one's emotions affect and contribute to, or detract from clear perceptions, logical or rational thought and successful actions. Also, at the level of assessment the distinction between proximate causes and more distant causes of one's ways of seeing, thinking and acting becomes interesting. An element of reflecting on reflecting may lead one to go beyond more obvious or easier to accept views of whatever 'works' as one operates.

Table 4:1 Dimensions of reflectivity

Level of vigour	Dimension of specificity		Dimension of depth or roundaboutness of causality	
	General	Specific (values emotions theory)	Surface/ immediate	Deep or more distant causality
Critique	Critiquing one's awareness which may lead to resolutions to change	Critiquing specific types of ways of seeing, thinking and acting which may also relate to emotional habits and conventional morality	Awareness that reasons why one should be critiquing one's ways of being are connected to particular events or situations in relation to other people	Taking awareness of one's situation to deeper levels i.e. aware of political and social and more generally of cultural setting
Assessment	Effective Efficient Acceptable	Emotional intelligence Ethical competence	Most obvious context (working, practicing a profession)	Broader context of culture or personal history and disposition
Awareness	of self in context of perception, thought and action	of aspects or ways of perceiving, thinking, acting		

At a more sophisticated but probably less frequently exercised level of reflection, one can take a critical attitude towards one's ways of seeing, thinking and acting. One could say that critique logically follows assessment. Again critique can be general or specific, depending on whether one has the conceptual tools to bundle ways of perceiving, thinking or acting in particular ways. Recently emotional intelligence has become a popular way of bundling ways of being. Other possibilities may relate to the distinction between technical and ethical competence or the distinction between building repertoires of thoughts or actions and calling up elements from those repertoires. A gun-slinger may know how to draw a gun quickly and may have practiced shooting tin cans lined up on a wall on cloudy days. He ought to reflect on whether he can do it quickly enough when the sun is in his eyes, or when confronted by someone who may be faster and therefore when he may be facing death. Also when one is taking a critical attitude towards one's way of being, there are differences in how widely, how deeply, how far back in one's history, one goes in order not only to assess what has gone wrong, but also to gain insight into what one might do to improve the situation. Clearly critical reflection would be stimulated by the gun-slinger getting wounded in a gun fight. Whether than leads him to change his technique, or give up wearing a gun, or to wear sunglasses depends on how deeply he reflects on his practice and not just on his action.

Reflective practice involves both levels and dimensions of reflectivity and aspects of practice. The way the practice aspect of reflective practice has been categorised is commonly according to whether the reflection occurs before, during or after practice or action. Above we consider more the depth of reflection both in terms of layers of reflection (reflecting on reflection; evaluating reflections on reflection) and in terms of degrees of criticality towards reflection.

4.4.2   Schön and reflective practice

Schön's develops what he calls the "epistemology of practice implicit in the artistic, intuitive processes which some practitioners bring to situations of uncertainty, instability, uniqueness and value conflict" (1983: 49). For this he develops the concept of "reflection-in-action", which involves knowing-in-action and reflecting-in-action.

Knowing-in-action – This relates to tacit knowing: "getting it, or having it". This concerns actions and activities that one can do spontaneously without having to think about 'it' before or during the performance of it. Some have learned and been aware of learning such things, but others just 'know', such as the way something feels in one's hand or the way one is aware that something is not quite right without being able to describe what right would be or feel like.

Ethical competence, like most forms of technical competence, will eventually be expressed primarily by knowing-in-action. That is, the experienced professional will generally know what to do as situations arise, because they have experienced situations which are close enough to the current one. It is likely that the professional involved will not even think of what they are doing as based on ethical competence. It will merely be a matter of doing what they feel is 'right'. This can be dangerous when a situation is confronted which is really different, or if ethical expectations of clients and the profession as a whole change. This is where reflection-in-action and reflection-in-practice become important.

The recent case of Blue Peter (children's television) staff who faked winning responses by children to a competition, rather than admitting that a technical fault had meant that no responses to the competition could be received in time for the allotted time that the winner was to be announced on air, is a very public example of the difference between knowing-in-action and reflecting-in-action as an ethically competent professional. The staff seem to have acted "spontaneously" and shown a facility for knowing-in-action that "the show must go on", whatever 'it' takes, rather than reflecting-in-action that it is wrong to lie and to try to dupe the viewing public.

Reflecting-in-action –This has been variously described as "thinking on your feet" or "learning by doing" or for a cricket player, "getting your eye in": "maintaining and developing it". An example is how a jazz musician makes adjustments to what they hear others are doing. The element of surprise can be important here as knowing-in-action is translated into knowledge-in-action. The key is that there is a feedback loop from actual conditions to how one adjusts in reaction to those conditions.

Concerning ethical competence, this involves dealing with non-standard situations or at least with situations unfamiliar to the practitioner. A deep ethical competence is needed to support professionals to reflect-in-action in such a manner as to reflect professional ethics as expressed through codes. The practice of reflecting-in-action should not be confined to 'ethical super-competents' or ethical 'experts' among the practitioners.

Reflecting-in-practice – This concerns what may be regarded as reflection before action. The experience of practice leads a professional to build a "repertoire of expectations, images and techniques". Stabilising practice reduces surprise and so knowing-in-practice becomes more tacit, spontaneous and automatic, which leads to benefits to the professional and to clients of specialization. There are dangers to this if professionals develop selective inattention to phenomena that do not fit and if they lose the overall picture by specialisation. This can be countered by reflection-after-practice as well as more conscious pursuit of reflection-in-action.

Reflection-after-practice – This was not a concept developed by Schön, and he has been criticised for leaving it out. In his defence, he was writing before the movement towards formalised CPD or CPE became a widespread feature of what professional associations offer to their members, and increasingly require of their members.

It is imperative that professional bodies provide or accredit opportunities for their members to undertake continuing professional training in ethical issues. There are many ways this can be done including providing specific courses and other materials on ethical dilemmas and the consequences of ethical incompetence. It could be connected to formal requirements for CPD. These issues are discussed in detail in Chapter 6.

4.5 Phases in the execution of ethical competence

Schön's distinctions concerning reflective practice concern aspects of what goes on during professional activity, and others have extended his views to include what can go on before and after professional activity or practice. These aspects of the timeliness of reflection for it to influence professional competence can be applied to ethical competence as well. Just as reflection may be considered in terms of phases associated with the action or activities of professional practice, so we can understand how ethical competence may be supported by considering a series of phases in relation to the exercise of professional action that is ethically competent. Four phases that can be distinguished are (see Jones, 2005):

- Perception

- Cognition

- Emotion

- Action.

First, individuals need to be able to be able to recognise a situation as one in which ethical competence is relevant. One needs to be sensitised to an issue as ethically relevant in order to perceive that any particular situation is one with an ethical dimension. Second, individuals need to have been socialised into thinking of themselves as ethically competent. This is clearly a role that professional associations take on and provide support for their members to think of themselves as ethically competent. They need to associate the concept with being a professional.

Third, one needs to feel morally aroused in a particular situation. One needs to exercise moral judgement, which may require an individual to eschew what is easy, or even what one may have done in the past in situations that are similar to the current one, but also different in that critical way that has led to it being perceived as one in which ethical competence is relevant.

Finally one needs to act in the right way. This will be affected by the need to overcome lethargy as well as competing pulls on one's sphere of action. Often it can be much easier not to act, such as in a situation when one ought to become a whistleblower.

- Part 2 -
Understanding the support professional bodies can provide for ethical competence

- Chapter 5 -
Supports for the Ethical Code

5.1   Introduction

The Ethical Code is a critical element in the definition of ethical competence for particular professions. It also may be viewed as a support for ethical competence, but one that needs further supports specific to it.

A code can support ethical competence. However, if it is not well known to clients and the general public, its influence in engendering trust towards the practitioners will be weakened. Worse still, if it is unclear and written in language that is arcane and familiar only to aficionados of the profession, it may have the opposite effect and breed suspicion towards practitioners. Even worse than these problems, if the code contains statements that are regarded as purely aspirational and if the general public believes that obligations set out in the code do not reflect actual practice, the code can lead to cynicism towards practitioners and be viewed as merely a public relations exercise by the profession. This situation is more likely to occur if members of the profession are not familiar with the code itself and if they do not understand the thinking behind the code. The code itself must be supported if it is to contribute to the ethical competence of practitioners and to a view among the general public that practitioners are trustworthy.

How can the code be 'supported' by professional associations? This can involve many different policies and activities.

- Making the code accessible to members of the profession, but just as important, we would argue, it should be accessible to the general public and particularly to clients, potential clients and employers of members of the profession.

- Clarifying the code, making it understandable by issuing more detailed guidelines, and offering other forms of clarification, such as the issuing of advice based on well known ethical dilemmas that involve code obligations.

- Being aware of and following principles of good code design, such as: ensuring consistency of statements in the code, clearly specifying to whom obligations are owed, ordering obligations in a useful manner (perhaps by degree of compulsion or strength of obligation).

- Keeping the code up-to-date.

- Providing opportunities for students to 'learn' the code and its implications for practice.

- Providing opportunities for practitioners to brush up on the code and its implications for practice through various forms of CPD.

The first four of these issues are dealt with in turn in the following sections of this chapter. The last two issues are dealt with in the next chapter.

The definition of a professional association used by PARN includes having, or making a commitment to having, an Ethical Code (in addition to having an educational or experience standard for admission, a policy commitment to continuing professional development and maintaining a register of members). This allows a wide definition of what can be included as a professional association. A few representative organisations for occupational groups and for areas of occupational expertise do not have Ethical Codes or continuing professional development policies, however, we know that they plan to develop them. For example, in the 2006 PARN survey of professional associations, 94% of the 110 UK respondents stated that the members of their organisation operate under a code that sets out the expected standards of professional behaviour. The percentage was comparable for the 21 Irish respondents, 95%. The same question was asked in the 2003 PARN survey. Of the 61 UK associations that answered both questionnaires (the 'matched sample') the percentage with a code had risen during the 3 years from 87% to 95%. That is, 5 respondents that had no code in 2003, had one in 2006. All 15 of the Irish associations that answered both questionnaires reported that they operate under an Ethical Code.

5.2 Accessibility of the code to members of the profession

The code needs to be readily available for members of the profession to refer to when faced with a situation that may involve an ethical dilemma. The code needs to clarify to practitioners the obligations they have in practice situations.

In the PARN surveys of professional associations in the UK and Ireland of 2006, respondents were asked if they provided positive support for awareness of ethical behaviour among their members. The results are shown in Table 5:1.

Table 5:1 Supports for member awareness of the Ethical Code and required ethical behaviour: 2006

Support for the Ethical Code within the profession: 2006 survey	UK	Ireland
Printed guidance	52%	60%
Articles in newsletters on ethical subjects	42%	50%
Telephone helpline	25%	40%
Guidance on website	52%	40%
Courses/seminars on ethics other than initial qualifications	22%	40%
Examples of ethically difficult situations	10%	15%
Other	7%	5%
Sample size	103	20

Of the 9 who ticked 'other' in the UK 8 associations specified what that meant. Of these 2 mentioned Ethics Forums and 2 said they provide telephone support if asked, but do not advertise it as a telephone helpline. One had an ethics committee that would provide advice to members when asked and 2 had what they termed "ethical counsellors" or "an independent confidential adviser on ethical and personal issues" available to members. One, and in addition the one association in Ireland that ticked other and specified what they meant, mentioned email communications on ethics or e-Bulletins sent to practitioners.

This question was asked in the 2003 survey as well as the 2006 survey. Table 5:2 compares the results for those that responded to both surveys in the UK.

Table 5:2 Supports for member awareness of the Ethical Code and required ethical behaviour: UK

Type of support for members of the profession	2003 survey	2006 survey
Printed Guidance	68%	54%
Telephone Helpline	29%	24%
Guidance on Website	39%	54%
Courses/seminars on ethics (other than in initial qualification)	25%	25%
Other	14%	14%
Sample size	59	59

There was a slight decline in the proportion offering telephone helplines and printed guidance. However there was a substantial increase in the proportion offering guidance on their websites. The options of articles in newspapers on ethical subjects and examples of ethically difficult situations were not offered in the 2003 survey. The proportion stating examples of ethically difficult subjects were included in 'other' for 2006.

As can be seen from Table 5:3, the pattern of change between 2003 and 2006 among the Irish associations that responded to both surveys was very similar to the UK pattern.

Table 5:3 Supports for member awareness of the Ethical Code and required ethical behaviour: Ireland

Type of support for members of the profession	2003 survey	2006 survey
Printed Guidance	53%	60%
Telephone Helpline	53%	48%
Guidance on Website	33%	40%
Courses/seminars on ethics (other than in initial qualification)	33%	33%
Other	7%	13%
Sample size	15	15

5.3 Case studies on supports for member awareness of the codes and general awareness of ethical competence issues: BMA, CIMA, ACCA

It is hardly surprising that ethics is a high priority for doctors and the professional body that regulates doctors, the General Medical Council (GMC). However as we have made clear in this book, support for ethical competence does not only come from investigating those that are suspected of falling below the standards required of technical and ethical competence, and of prosecuting those for whom suspicions have been proved. The British Medical Association (BMA) provides a wide range of positive support for the ethical competence of doctors. The case study presented here emphasises the role of the ethics advisory services of the BMA. It is notable that this advisory service is also aimed at one set of stakeholders of the medical profession as well as the doctors themselves; that is, government advisors developing medical policy.

Accounting professional associations in the UK are particularly active in supporting ethical competence of their members. However their approaches are not the same as demonstrated by the two further case studies in this section. The Chartered Institute of Management Accountants (CIMA) has concentrated responsibility for ethical competence support in a full-time ethics manager. The Association of Certified Chartered Accountants (ACCA) has been developing animated simulations of ethical dilemmas, and ethics micro site on their website and they have surveyed their members on ethical attitudes. The Institute of Chartered Accountants in England and Wales (ICAEW) have also recently redesigned their code (we include a case study on ICAEW in Chapter 6 focusing on their educational activities and disciplinary procedures).

Case study 5.1
Based on an interview with Julian Sheather - Senior Ethics Advisor, British Medical Association.

The British Medical Association (BMA) represents over 139,000 doctors in the UK. Their role is not to regulate ethical practice; that is the job of the General Medical Council (GMC), but to provide ethics advisory services to both its members and to those developing medical policy. "Good medical practice is ethical practice".

The BMA considers its role in regard to ethics to be one of ensuring the highest standards of ethical practice amongst doctors. As Julian Sheather suggests, high standards of clinical care are not possible without ethical knowledge; ethics is at the core of the practice of medicine. Consequently, the duty to inform and educate BMA members on ethical issues is taken extremely seriously.

The BMA have a dedicated ethics helpline; members can contact the Association by email, phone, or post with ethical dilemmas. Dedicated Ethics Advisors will then assist the doctors by talking them through the issue in order to try to reach a satisfactory conclusion. Part of this process, Julian says, is to identify the issue as an ethical one, before recognizing which ethical principles underlie the dilemma. The helpline is well used, with the ethics team dealing with around 6-10 queries a day. "We're seeing increasing recognition of the importance of medical ethics as being at the centre of good medical practice".

In terms of educating their members on ethics, the BMA Ethics Advisors produce ethics guidance to be published on the website. The purpose in this regard is to "elaborate on and develop" the often quite concise guidance offered by the GMC. A handbook has also recently been published, which presents case-studies and advice covering the majority of medical and professional ethics issues that doctors are likely to face. Journal articles covering ethics issues are written, and lectures on ethics are given to various groups from students to established GPs, in some cases as part of CPD courses run by external providers. The BMA Ethics department also works with the Press Office to cover any news features related to medical ethics.

The Ethics team is also involved in lobbying decision-makers where legislation is being produced which has an impact on medical ethics. The BMA, being a well-established voice in medical ethics issues, is in a good position to lobby on behalf of doctors.

Medical Ethics Committee
The BMA's Medical Ethics Committee is a key group in formulating the Association's ethics policies, and generally providing a 'steer' on ethics in the BMA, and the medical profession in general. The committee concentrates on issues arising in medical ethics, but there is clear overlap with professional ethics that would be relevant for other professions, such as issues of dual loyalties and confidentiality. The committee comprises doctors, philosophers, lawyers, theologians and lay people, and its role includes:

- Overseeing the ethical guidance produced by the BMA Ethics department;

- Looking at new and emerging ethical issues facing the medical profession, and how to address these issues;

- Shaping longer term BMA policy and strategy on ethics.

Case study 5.2
Based on an interview with Danielle Cohen - Ethics Manager, The Chartered Institute of Management Accountants.

The Chartered Institute of Management Accountants (CIMA) is unusual in having appointed an Ethics Manager. Danielle Cohen is the first Ethics Manager, appointed in May 2005, in response to the increased attention directed towards ethics and the need to have one particular employee responsible for ethics in order to successfully promote and integrate ethics into other areas of the organisation. Accountancy bodies in general have had Ethical Codes and guidelines for a number of years but there is a sense that they have been pushed higher up on the agenda, following high profile corporate scandals such as ENRON. Danielle believes there are different methods of promoting ethics, depending on the specifics of the organisation. However she commented:

> *What we were finding at CIMA was that if we were going to make the impact we wanted to in the area of ethics, we needed to have one person whose specific responsibility was to promote ethics to members.*

Since her appointment CIMA has developed partnerships with other organisations working in the area of ethics, such as the Institute of Business Ethics. They have a subscription agreement with *Public Concern at Work,* an independent charity who provide whistle-blowing advice lines for their members. They have also revised the Code of Ethics, the new one having come into effect in January 2006, replacing the old CIMA ethical guidelines. To go along with this and in order to promote ethics and support members' understanding of the new code, CIMA has introduced the following services:

- Ethics road shows

- Case studies in the newsletter

- Branch events

- A searchable CD-ROM of the Code of Ethics document

- Explanatory articles

- An ethics support package

The CD-ROM can be automatically updated and has been sent out to all members and students as well as being placed on the website. The ethics support package includes an ethics advice line, the whistle-blowing advice line and a legal advice line.

Prior to January 2006, the ethics guidelines had not been updated since 1992. The revision of the Code of Ethics was prompted by the new code introduced by the International Federation of Accountants (IFAC), of which CIMA are a member. As a member they were obliged to be compliant with this code but had also had some input into the writing of this code, being a member of the Consultative Committee of Accounting Bodies (CCAB). Sitting on the CCAB, with the five other major UK accountancy bodies, who incidentally all also revised their codes at that time, was beneficial for CIMA in developing the ethics programme: "On the CCAB ethics working party we end up benchmarking and knowing what each other are doing in the area."

The new code is divided into three parts; the first establishing the fundamental principles of ethics for professional accountants; integrity, objectivity, professional competence and due care, confidentiality and professional behaviour; the second illustrating specific situations that would apply to professional accountants in public practice; and the third, situations that would apply to professional accountants in business.

CIMA's CPD scheme recognises the need for developing ethical competencies and in order to do this they are in the process of developing an online ethics module comprising a series of case studies to work through.

The support systems are constantly monitored and modified according to the results of member surveys every two years. In terms of the code, while there are no specific plans to revise it currently, they intend to develop it in the future so that they can begin to target members' specific needs, particularly for those who work in business, which differs from other CCAB accounting institutes.

Case study 5.3
Based on interviews with Sundeep Takwani - Head of Ethics and Assurance and Margot Menzies - Head of Projects, Association of Certified Chartered Accountants.

The Association of Chartered Certified Accountants (ACCA) is the largest and fastest-growing global professional accountancy body with 296,000 students and 115,000 members in 170 countries. ACCA is a member of the International Federation of Accountants (IFAC), and its Ethical Code, which is reviewed on an annual basis, is closely aligned to the IFAC Code of Ethics. The benefit of this is that the Ethical Codes of different accountancy bodies are very similar to one another, providing a high level of consistency for accountants who may be members of more than one professional association. In the UK, ACCA meets other senior professional bodies in the accountancy sector in the CCAB Ethics Group, which enable collective and coordinated working on ethical matters as and when appropriate.

ACCA's Code of Ethics and Conduct is reviewed by the Professional Standards Directorate on a annual basis and is then ratified by Council. ACCA's Code applies to all members wherever they are based. "ACCA has a responsibility to act in the public interest, and members also need to share in that responsibility."

Historically, ethics has been hugely important for the accountancy sector, as it has been necessary to demonstrate strength in reacting to crises in the profession such as ENRON. Sundeep highlighted the fact that a distinguishing mark of the accountancy profession is its acceptance of the responsibility to act in the public interest, and under-pinning this is that members' responsibility to the public outweighs their responsibilities towards individual clients or employers.

The profession has steered the accountancy sector Codes of Ethics away from lists of things that the individual member can and can't do towards principles based codes, where it is not merely the case of just ticking a box and saying "I've met that example." As Sundeep says, it is "much broader than that." Legislation governing accountancy is also now principles-based. "Ethics cuts through everything we do."

When the Code of Ethics is revised, ACCA publishes articles in the members' newsletter to inform members of the changes. If the change impacts on a particular industry then ACCA publicises it through one of its sector-specific journals. The ethics section of the ACCA website is also a key tool in keeping levels of awareness of ethics high amongst members.

In 2006, a survey asking members about their ethical attitudes, and "what ethical issues they face in the workplace" was undertaken in conjunction with the Institute of Business Ethics, in order to maintain awareness of ethics amongst members. There was a good response rate to the survey, and some ethical dilemmas which can be used as case-studies were highlighted by members. There is also an ethics section in the routine member satisfaction surveys carried out by ACCA.

Ethics micro-site
The ethics section of the ACCA website is integral to ensuring the wide availability of ethics resources for members. It can be found in the CPD section of the ACCA website, thus emphasising the links between CPD and ethics.

The resources that are provided via the website include:

- Information and guidance on the Ethical Code

- Online ethics courses, including bespoke modules on the Code of Ethics

- Ethics news stories

- Searchable ethics case studies.

ACCA is currently trialing animated simulations that put people in ethical situations. It is hoped that these simulations will assist members' professional ethical development by allowing people to experience ethical dilemmas and make judgments. "Ethics is part of our core qualification, it's what we expect members to have."

Ethics is at the heart of the ACCA qualification syllabus currently under development and will meet the IFAC education standard on the understanding of ethical dilemmas. Part of the ethics education process is about how to identify ethical issues in the first place.

Further ethics support offered by ACCA includes the facility for members to email or phone its Advisory Services Section to discuss their particular ethical dilemmas.

The University of Glasgow who are setting up an Ethics Centre has also approached ACCA, along with other professional associations. The aim is, as Margo explains, to "bring employers and academia together on ethics".

Sundeep finally suggests that any successful Code of Ethics has to be linked to robust procedures for dealing with unethical behaviour, In the case of ACCA, the ultimate sanction is removal from ACCA. ACCA's Disciplinary Committee, which deals with cases where members have failed to observe proper standards of professional conduct, is a public forum; "anyone could turn up and watch", and it is formed by a majority of lay-people.

5.4 Accessibility of the code to members of the public

While it is important for the code to be accessible to practitioners in order for them to understand the obligations they have in practice situations, it is arguably equally important for the general public to be able to access the code to discover what they can expect from a practitioner in that profession.

In the PARN Professionalisation of Professional Associations Survey of 2006, respondents were asked if they take steps to promote awareness of their Ethical Code beyond their own members; for example to potential clients, the general public or employers. Most associations in the UK, 59% responded positively (sample size 103) and a higher proportion did so in Ireland, 80% (sample size 20).

This hardly changed between the two surveys. For the UK matched sample, 59% responded positively both in 2003 and in 2006 (sample size 59) and in Ireland the proportion rose from 73% in 2003 to 80% in 2006 (sample size 15).

If respondents responded yes to taking steps to promote awareness of their code beyond their own members, they were then asked if those steps included any of a listed set of actions or policies. The percentages reported are of the whole sample, at least those who responded to the first part of the question, whether positively or negatively. Respondents were asked to tick all options that applied to them:

Table 5:4 Supports for public awareness of the Ethical Code and required ethical behaviour: 2006

Type of publicity for members of the public: 2006	UK	Ireland
Available on homepage of the website	35%	70%
Leaflets available for public/clients	31%	40%
Compulsory reference by professional to client (as in contracts)	8%	30%
Other	18%	15%
Sample size	100	20

Of the 18 in the UK who ticked 'other' and specified what this meant;

- 10 said it was on the website, but not on the homepage.

- 2 stated that it was mentioned in the annual register of members.

- 1 mentioned that the Ethical Code is referred to in articles in publications in their own sector as well as those of their members' clients and another mentioned advertising and other publications and a third mentioned PR information.

- 1 mentioned talks to groups.

- 1 stated that they recommend that agencies refer to their compliance with professional association regulations at the pitch/tender stage.

- The remaining 3 specified how they provide information to their members rather than the general public.

One of those who said it was on their website, but not on the homepage specifically said that it is included in a directory of members, but that it "needs moving to more prominent place on website".

Of the 3 Irish associations that ticked other, 2 said it was mentioned in advertising and 1 stated that there was a "disclaimer only on website". It was recommended in the recent PARN publication on Ethical Codes (Friedman et al., 2005), that accessibility to the public should be enhanced by the code being no more than two clicks away from the home page of all professional associations. This is a simple test that can be carried out.

It is encouraging that there is some evidence that techniques for making codes more accessible outside the profession are becoming more widespread, even if only slowly. Only the options of leaflets and required reference to the code by their members in client relations were offered in 2003. For the UK the proportion of the matched sample providing these things rose slightly from 2003 to 2006. Compulsory reference to the code in client relations rose from 6% to 8% and leaflets available for public/clients rose from 31% to 35% (sample size 48). For the Irish sample the same proportion had the policy of requiring reference to the code by members in their client relations, but the proportion making leaflets available for public/clients rose from 33% in 2003 to 50% in 2006 (sample size 12).

A related issue is whether associations have a client service charter or similar public statement, setting out the standards of service that clients, customers or patients should expect from professional service providers. A fairly substantial 24% of UK respondents replied positively to this, as did 29% of Irish respondents.

5.5 Case study on promoting ethics activities of an association to the wider public: BCS

The new Ethics Forum recently established by the British Computer Society (BCS) provides an interesting approach to widening understanding of what that society is doing to support the ethical competence of IT specialists.

Case study 5.4
Based on an interview with Mike Rodd – Director, The British Computer Society

The British Computer Society (BCS) has had an Ethics Expert Panel in place for over a decade, in recognition that its role as a chartered body, awarding chartered status, requires a "living" code of (professional) conduct. Also, in line with the Quality Assurance Agency's Benchmark for Computing and as an academic accrediting body, BCS is obliged to follow the requirement that all degree courses in the subject should contain a component of ethics in IT. In January 2007 the Ethics Expert Panel was replaced by a new Ethics Forum, adding to the six other Forums dealing with different, society-wide issues, already in existence in BCS. This came about due to the increasing view in BCS that ethics is a fundamental issue for the IT profession. As Mike Rodd the Director commented: "ethics has a far more important role than ever in the IT profession and if anything, ethical behaviour underpins the IT profession."

Increasing attention towards ethics in IT has been stimulated by media attention directed towards privacy and confidentiality issues in new initiatives such as the introduction of ID cards and a new NHS computer system, allowing patient records to be accessed more quickly and easily. The press has become increasingly interested in the reasons behind failures in IT systems and the lack of whistle-blowing in the IT profession.

The new Ethics Forum was introduced in order to increase the profile of the work BCS does on ethics and to attract senior members of the industry and academia to work for them in this area. They now employ a part-time manager of this Forum who also teaches ethics outside BCS. The Ethics Forum has entirely taken on the responsibilities of the old Ethics Expert Panel, including the code of conduct and code of good practice. In addition, it now has complete responsibility for advice on possible new activities in the ethics area, and new content in this area for degree syllabuses.

BCS found PARN's annual conference last year very useful, in order to become aware of what other professional bodies were doing in this area, when designing the Forum. BCS does have a disciplinary process in place, if members do not comply with the code of conduct, but the Forum itself does not deal with infractions by members:

Our Trustees believe absolutely implicitly that the disciplinary process has to be separated from the body that creates the rules of discipline. In other words, the body creating the code of conduct cannot be responsible for implementing it.

Given that the Forum is still in its infancy, it does not yet specifically deal with members' ethical dilemmas. Members with any ethical problems would go through more senior members of the society and then seek legal advice if needed. However BCS hope to provide support for members directly from the Forum in future.

When introducing the Ethics Forum, BCS encountered few problems because the Ethics Expert Panel had been in place for some years. One of the keys to the success of their Panel was the decision to go outside their membership to get the expertise needed. This has been replicated on the Forum. The other vital lesson learnt was that in order to succeed with this kind of initiative, commitment from the top is vital:

To rely totally on volunteers is just not going to work; it's too technical and too complicated, with legal implications. To develop a code of conduct certainly requires a lot of volunteer effort, but also internal, professional support.

BCS acknowledge that there is still a lot more work to be done in this area. Mike sees it as vital that the image of IT Professionals as being unethical is challenged. The ethical support systems in BCS are a fundamental step towards this. Services that he would like to introduce in the future, include support for whistle-blowers and monitoring of competence and qualifications amongst IT professionals. BCS also has a number of staff who work with politicians in government and whose role it is to talk to the media and try to increase public awareness of the problems and issues involved in IT, such as data protection and security.

5.6   Principles of good code design

Beyond accessibility, Friedman et al, (2005) offer three further principles of good code design: clarity, consistency and comprehensiveness. The principles of good design of codes can be implemented by revisions to the code. Revising codes can be a useful exercise not only to improve their design, but also to develop content in response to changes in priorities within the profession. As we will show in the section that follows this, a surprisingly high proportion of professional bodies have carried out revisions to professional codes in recent years.

5.6.1   Clarity and the code

Clarity is discussed in relation to the understandability and precision of the terms involved. We recommend considering plain English and avoiding general calls to "be professional" or to "be of good character". Also we recommend clear specification of the beneficiaries to whom obligations are owed for each separate type of obligation, avoiding duplication and consideration of a principle by which to order the statements in the code, perhaps by beneficiaries or by level of compulsion in the language. Another recommendation is to include a preamble in the code.

Ethical Codes often begin with a short preamble and PARN recommends this in order to clarify whether the code is primarily aspirational or if it will be used as a basis for judging misconduct and to ascertain whether members should remain on the register of the professional body. A statement reminding the public and members that all members on the register have agreed to abide by the code is useful. There are different purposes a code fulfils and it is useful to make it clear at the outset which of the following purposes the particular code is meant to serve: inform members of standards expected of them, inform the public as to what they should expect from members, guide fitness to practice panels or perhaps merely to inform potential members of what the profession stands for (though PARN is concerned that if this last purpose is all the code is meant to do, it will harm, rather than help, the standing and trust given to that profession).

Also a preamble can be useful to explain the design of the code or any other aspect of the code that may seem unusual, for example, if the code is thin in a particular area because further statements in that area are included in a more detailed guidelines. Also for some professional bodies there may be some confusion as to which code applies to whom. This can occur when association and regulator are separate or where there is more than one regulatory body in the field.

5.6.2   Consistency and the code

A range of inconsistencies were found in the codes analysed by Friedman et al. (2005). It was found that many codes had seemingly random variations in the level of abstraction of statements; some to do with general values or character traits and some with specific aspects of conduct. PARN recommends that these should be ordered in some way. There were also inconsistencies in the degree of compulsion indicated. Some codes contained statements like "members must at all times..." sprinkled among statements like "members should...". It was not clear that these inconsistencies were intended and what they meant for practitioners. In addition there were some statements in the code that could be mistaken for simple job specifications or descriptions of practice, rather than obligations for practitioners.

5.6.3   Comprehensiveness and the code

PARN argues that comprehensiveness, or at least a serious attempt at being comprehensive, is important in the design of Ethical Codes. Newer codes tend to be more comprehensive because newer occupations to professionalise tend to be more open to benchmarking themselves against others. The range of beneficiaries tends to be wider in these codes as well as the range of types of obligations. More traditional professions would do well to examine these codes when they decide to revise their own codes. The 'Matrix' model presented in Friedman et al. (2005) allows this to be done without a huge effort.

5.7 Pressures to keep codes up-to-date

5.7.1 Pressures to keep the code up-to-date

Some pressures to update codes come from a determination to make them more accessible. Codes meant to be read by people other than those within the profession need to be written in an accessible manner. This is a general pressure reflecting the change in attitude towards all professions to 'earn' trust rather than expect 'blind trust' will be forthcoming.

Other pressures for changing codes reflect the changing environment of individual professions. Codes are coming to be viewed as more public documents than in the past.[17] Nowadays there is an expectation that changes in the environment of associations will lead to changes in their codes as a signal to the general public that obligations have changed or are being formulated in different ways. This can be occasioned by many factors, such as:

- Legislative frameworks. On one hand, new legislation can emerge from previously separate jurisdictions, such as the introduction of new EU legislation affecting the regulation of professional associations in individual member states. Other changes come from new social pressures as they are formulated in legislation, such as new environmental legislation. This may not directly impinge on a particular profession. Such legislation may be aimed directly at private companies. However, the sensitivity of professions to support new requirements on their employers and the general increase in social sensitivity towards these issues leading to changing social norms, come to be reflected in the codes of those professions particularly concerned with issues that

---

[17] There was a time towards the end of the 19th and the beginning of the 20th Century when codes were being developed by new professions which were meant to be public statements. However from the mid to late 20th Century, with the rise of public sector professions, having a public code was less emphasised. These new professions were 'protected' from the public by their employer being the State and therefore having legitimacy derived from that source rather than, or at least requiring less legitimacy from, occupational expertise.

may lead to environmental damage. In addition the new legislation may encourage professionalisation of new occupational groups, both in terms of expanding their market and encouraging them to distinguish themselves from others competing for that market.

- Regulatory frameworks. In the UK, regulatory functions (or at least those concerned with complaints and discipline) are being separated from previously self-regulating professional associations. The most notable case is the Law Society of England and Wales, from which both the Solicitors Regulatory Authority and a new complaints authority have been separated. New specialist regulatory bodies are likely to develop new codes for the profession.

- Competition from other professions or from new professions wanting to encroach on a particular profession's jurisdiction. This is the primary pressure on professional associations according to Abbott (1988), though we regard it as only one of many, and one that occupies most professional associations only infrequently.

- Break ups or spin offs from a professional association as former special interest groups or sections detach themselves, stimulating a change in code for both the remainder as well as the emerging group. We regard this as more common than head-to-head confrontations between proximate professional groups. It occurs because the accumulation of more detailed knowledge in professional fields commonly leads to new techniques being used most intensively by subsections of professions. This can be regarded as a distinguishing characteristic of these practitioners. It can lead them to have different concerns both in relation to their ethical competence as well as their technical competence. It can encourage them to regard themselves as a different profession altogether from their colleagues.. These tensions exist in most professions. How they are dealt with varies. Many are contained by sensitive support provided by the central headquarters to the professional body's disparate groups. However this can be an unstable situation, particularly if a catalytic event occurs which throws up the differences in approaches to practice or the feeling among the minority that the professional association is insufficiently sensitive to their position and their needs.

- Mergers and takeovers among professional associations can encourage the new entity to make a public statement of its presence and to distinguish it from the past entities. This can be stimulated by jurisdictional competition, but also by legislative and regulatory change. Concerning the latter, there are pressures on professional bodies to merge, coming from government agencies who manage aspects of what the professional bodies do. For example, the UK government has set up English Heritage. It deals with a broad range of professions concerned with heritage from traditionally very different fields of knowledge: archaeology, building conservation, conservation of artefacts (which have traditionally been distinguished by the nature of the raw material of the artefacts considered: wood, cloth, metals etc). If a new heritage profession were to emerge, the codes of the component professions making it up will have to be melded together in some way. It may also occasion new obligations and new beneficiaries of obligations being explicitly named in the new code due to the changed position of this collection of professions.

5.7.2   Reasons to up-date codes, certain aspects of codes and different ways it can be done

There are many reasons to revise a professional Ethical Code. In the previous section we described general features of the environment affecting professions that may stimulate a change in professional code. Here we examine more detailed aspects of changes in the situations of professional bodies as they directly affect different aspects of codes that may be changed.

First, many codes have been written in archaic language and need to be rewritten not only to be more clearly understood by students in the profession, but also by the general public as potential clients of the profession. Terms that are clear only to those in the practice of the profession will need to be removed or explained in the code. The nature syntax and grammar of the code may need updating if the code was last revised centuries ago. Also many codes reflect a formal legalese that characterises Royal Charters, which celebrate their ancient language or regard it as a legitimator.

Second, the nature of obligations changes with changes to the context of the profession. For example, whistle-blowing has become a new obligation required of many professions. Obligations to restrict advertising have been relaxed.

Third, a wider range of beneficiaries of obligations has emerged. As more professions emerge from deepening division of labour on one hand, and as the need to recombine professional services grows from technical developments that cross professional fields of knowledge, there is a greater need for teamwork among professionals. This has led several professional bodies to include obligations to related professions and to whomever a professional works with on a team or collegial bases even if they are not members of the same profession or professional body. This has become particularly common in the health sector. Also there is a new-found notion among many, particularly medical, professional bodies that a professional owes some obligation to one's self. This would seem to go against the type of obligation regarded by many professional bodies as critical for professionalism, which is selflessness. For some academics, this has been a key mark of the professional, disinterest or lack of self-interest or the service ideal. However, it is recognised that in some professions this can go too far, with particularly junior doctors working too many hours or levels of suicide being too high for medical general practitioners.

5.8 Experiences of keeping the code up-to-date: re-legitimisation

Codes in the past have been revised. A flurry of this activity seems to occur whenever there are major changes in the legislative framework surrounding codes. In these circumstances it is common for the revisions to be carried out by individuals or small committees, guided by legal experts as well as those with long experience in practice, often past presidents or chairs of Council. However a relatively new trend is for revisions to involve widespread consultation within the profession. This we regard as good practice, as more likely to lead to greater compliance with the code, if the profession as a whole has a say in the revised codes.

Overall almost half, 49%, of UK respondents to the 2006 PARN survey had reviewed their Ethical Code within the past 2 years and 61% had reviewed their code in the past 3 years. In addition almost a third, 30% stated that they planed to review their code in the next 12 months. This is a truly impressive picture. The Irish were even more likely to have carried out revisions to their code in the 12 months before the 2006 survey. In addition a surprising 53% stated they plan to revise their code in the next 12 months after the 2006 survey.

The picture was even more impressive in 2003. Table 5:5 compares these results on the matched sample of 59 that answered both surveys in the UK and 15 that did so in Ireland.

Table 5:5   Timings for revising Ethical Codes of professional associations[18]

	UK		Ireland	
Revision to code:	2003 survey	2006 survey	2003 survey	2006 survey
Planned in the next 12 months	32%	29%	33%	53%
Carried out in past 12 months	31%	25%	40%	33%
Carried out in past 1-2 years	25%	20%	20%	7%
Carried out in past 2-3 years	12%	17%	13%	7%
Not carried out in past 3 years	22%	36%	27%	53%
Sample size	59	59	15	15

Among the UK sample reviewing the Ethical Code was a common experience of the recent past, with 45% of the matched sample having carried out revisions in the two years from the summer of 2004 up to the summer of 2006 and 29% planning to make revisions in the year to summer 2007, the comparable figures for the three years between 2002 to 2004 were 56% and 32%. The figures do not tally. In 2003 32% of associations said they planned to carry out revisions in the next 12 months, that is 2003-2004, but only 17% in the 2006 survey stated that they carried out revisions to their code in the past 2-3 years; that would have been 2003-2004. The situation is even more inconsistent with the Irish sample with 33% stating in 2003 that they planned to carry out revisions in the next 12 months, but only 7% stating in 2006 that they had carried out revisions to the code in the past 2-3 years. Presumably this is either because all who planned to make revisions within the next 12 months in 2003 may not have succeeded in keeping to the plan or keeping to the timetable, or because all revisions to the code during 2003-2004 may not have been remembered in 2006.

---

[18] Note that the UK figures for revisions in the past do not add up to 100% because all of the matched sample did not have codes. Note also that the proportion of the UK matched sample not having codes was higher in 2003 than in 2006.

Nevertheless, the results of the survey show widespread activity in code revision during the first years of the twenty-first century. We suspect that if the same questions had been asked in the 1990s and particularly in the 1950s-80s, much less activity would have been recorded. It also seems that the extent of this activity has become a little less widespread recently, though still very common. Just taking what are likely to be the most reliable figures, those for revisions carried out in the last 12 months, the figures for both the UK and Ireland are very impressive.

5.9 Cases studies on revising the code: ICE, ISTC

Gathering information about what other professional associations have done can be very useful when an association comes to revise its code. This does not mean that codes of other associations, even those in closely related professions, should be simply copied. Rather the information gathered needs to be reflected upon in order to help those charged with revising the code decide what is appropriate for their own practitioners. The two case studies presented here provide a perspective on how general tools developed to help associations to revise their codes must be adapted to specific conditions of individual associations.

Case study 5.5
Based on an interview with Paul Taylor - Clerk to the Professional Conduct Panel, The Institution of Civil Engineers.

In July 2004 the Institution of Civil Engineers (ICE) revised its rules of professional conduct, producing a new document, the 'Code of Professional Conduct'. An ethics sub-committee was set up specifically to deal with the revisions to the rules, which comprised Fellows of the Institution who had had experience on the ICE professional conduct panel or the ICE disciplinary board. Their primary aim was to cover areas where there had been misconduct or complaints in the past. As Paul Taylor, Clerk to the Professional Conduct Panel, commented: "The primary driver was a need to produce a code that was relevant to today's profession and to protect the public interest."

The ICE consulted members when producing the code. They sent out a first draft to members, inviting their comments; placed an article in the institution's magazine and advertised it on the website. As well as consulting members, the ICE also examined codes of conduct from many other major institutions in the UK and from civil engineering professional bodies in several other countries worldwide. The code from New Zealand became the main model for the ICE's final code. When the final version was complete, it was put to the ICE Council for final approval.

The new code took into account the Engineering Council's guidelines. The rules of conduct contained in the code were simplified from 16 rules to six, with guidance notes for each one, abandoning rules that had become irrelevant or obsolete. As a separate exercise the previous year, the ICE had also amended its by-laws to make it compliant with the recent human rights legislation, giving any member who had been found guilty of improper conduct the right to appeal to an impartial and independent tribunal.

The biggest difficulty encountered in writing the new code was to ensure that the rules would be actually enforceable. Rule 4 of the code ("All members shall show due regard for the environment and for the sustainable management of natural resources"), proved especially difficult in this respect as it is less tangible than the others. It resulted in guidance on sustainability and the environment appearing in a separate document, 'Advice on Ethical Conduct' that the Ethics Sub-committee produced at the same time as the new Code. This document contained additional, mainly non-mandatory guidance on ethical conduct.

A copy of the rules of conduct contained in the new code was sent to all members in 2005, and the rules are explained on the website. There is also a contact number for advice on the application of the rules. However there has been little member feedback since the code was introduced other than a small number of specific enquiries. Paul puts this down to the success of the code and its presentation in clear, comprehensible language.

There is a requirement for the professional qualification that members have an understanding and knowledge of the code, which they are questioned on. The new code was not developed as part of a larger CPD scheme, but there is a realisation that this needs to be considered in more detail in the future. In common with other engineering institutions, the ICE has come to perceive ethical competence as a central part of the profession rather than just an add-on.

Case study 5.6
Based on an interview with Marian Newell - Journal Editor, The Institute of Scientific and Technical Communicators

The Institute of Scientific and Technical Communicators (ISTC) is a specialist organisation with about 800 individual members and 20 business affiliates. They have recently rewritten their Code of Ethics using, in part, PARN research as guidance. Marian Newell whose primary role is that of Journal Editor, took on this task in 2006. She was elected as a member of the Council in 2001 and, having experience in writing on an ethics-related topic for her MA dissertation, became responsible for promoting ethics within the organisation.

The ISTC became a member of PARN in 2005 and used our two books on the subject of ethics, *The Ethical Codes of UK Professional Associations* (2002) and *Analysing Ethical Codes of UK Professional Bodies* (2005), as a prompt for the revision of the code. Together with this, the Council was involved in a disciplinary hearing in 2002-2003 which revealed shortcomings in the existing code, and the new Chair of the Marketing Steering Group, appointed in late 2004, identified these further. The Code of Ethics was seen by the institute to be long, imprecise, old-fashioned and difficult to understand. Marian's aim for the new code was:

> *A pragmatic approach that seeks to inform members what the ISTC aspires to achieve, with the hope of inspiring better behaviour, rather than a pseudo legal document that would be difficult to enforce in reality.*

The ISTC found PARN's books beneficial, mainly by being reassured that they had considered all the issues. The examples of existing codes and the 'Matrix' for analysing codes in the books helped them to recognise that their existing code was extremely repetitive and did not cover all relevant aspects. The ISTC made a strategic decision to write a new code from scratch rather than revamping the existing one, enabling them to make the whole style simpler and the content more specific to general business practice. One difficulty was creating a balance between accessibility and formality: "we wanted something that people would read and buy into, but we weren't sure if removing the formality and legal language from the original would make the new code impossible to enforce."

The ISTC also faced the problem of how specific to make the new code. There is a risk of being too specific and missing out something vital. In this way, an all-encompassing code could become too lengthy or legalistic. On the other hand, Marian's advice to other organisations would be to make their code *"profession-specific"*, focusing particularly on the sector of the organisation and the particular needs of members, and concentrating on problems that are relevant to that type of business. The main idea drawn from the PARN publications was to clarify who the beneficiaries of clauses were, in order to make the idea of ethics more personal than abstract. As a result, the new Code of Ethics was organised as a series of duties to the following parties:

- The Institute

- The profession

- Clients or employers

- Peers and colleagues

- Users

- Suppliers

The rewrite also led to greater emphasis on copyright, intellectual property and accuracy rather than finance, contracts and gifts, which were found to be less relevant in this profession.

The review of the code was announced in the journal and newsletter, with detailed articles explaining particular points. A draft was also posted on the website in an attempt to get members' input. Very little feedback was received. Marian puts this down to the fact that ethical conflicts are not a major issue in technical communication but notes that they receive very little feedback in other areas as well. The lack of membership feedback is something that the ISTC would have liked to address when reviewing their code, possibly by creating a separate committee or even commissioning an external consultant: "It's hard to say you've got a mandate for anything because you know, while nobody's said they're not happy with it, nobody's said they are happy with it either."

The ISTC's disciplinary procedure is broken down into stages: suspension, downgrading, warning and apology. However, in the very few cases that have come to light since the new code was put in place, the code has not been called upon heavily. One example was related to the role of an editor in resolving conflicts between the requirements of author and publisher: "That kind of thing's really quite complex and legal. I find it difficult to envisage how an ethics code could have really helped because the problem was so specific...I don't feel that it's watertight."

The ISTC Council is considering introducing a mentoring service in the near future, which may include support on ethical issues. Other than that, periodic review of the code is the only solid plan in place, given the ISTC's size and resources.

- Chapter 6 -
Educating for ethical competence: IPQ and CPD

6.1   Introduction

The Ethical Codes of professional bodies can be regarded as the guides to ethical competence for those professions. However the content of codes is both more and less than ethical competence. It is more in the sense that the codes deal with issues that are broader than ethical competence, such as doing things that are expected of good citizens, things more like the first 5 of Gert's 10 moral rules as described in Chapter 2. Such issues may be regarded as a basis for ethical competence and are implied in codes under broad headings such as obligations to work within the framework of the law, rather than ethical competence itself. They may be thought of as representing issues relevant for avoiding ethical incompetence or ethical culpability. These are issues that one might be surprised to find in an Ethical Code, but are there sometimes because of past ethical problems for that profession, such as problems when there are discrepancies between the law in different countries and certain professional practices involve cross border services.

On the other hand, ethical competence will involve more specific and detailed understanding of how to behave or conduct oneself than can be covered in what are generally rather short documents. For example, simply stating that doctors or surveyors should act within the limits of their competence hardly provides sufficient guidance if some of these professionals are acting near the limit of the knowledge base of their speciality, or even of the entire field defined by the profession, and are therefore operating, or could be operating, at the limit of their own competence.   In these circumstances professionals need to decide at what point they will pass a patient or client on to others, or to call in additional support for their own judgement.   At the limit of the profession's knowledge base there is unlikely to be a hard and fast boundary to guide these decisions. Therefore even guidance notes to codes may not be detailed enough to support professionals in all situations when they should demonstrate ethical competence.

How can professionals gain an understanding of when it is appropriate to act in certain ways and when not, in circumstances which are unusual or particularly uncertain and complex? Furthermore, can professional training encourage individuals to make the right choices when temptation is put in their way: not to cheat, deceive or lie, not to carry out actions which they suspect or know are not in the best interests of their clients or others to whom obligations are owed, when they are under pressure to perform or to come up to expectations to provide clear answers for clients/patients? What are professional bodies doing to encourage ethical competence through education and training? Before going on to deal with this last question we begin with a discussion of ethical theory in relation to what may be the more effective methods of educating for ethical competence. We then examine current policies of professional associations to support the ethical competence of their members, first in relation to initial professional qualifications and then in relation to continuing professional development. We then go on to discuss aspects of the content of education for ethical competence.

6.2 Approaches to educating for ethical competence: deontological vs virtue ethics

Two different approaches to ethics education, based on the distinct philosophies of ethics described in Chapter 2, have been influential: deontological and virtue ethics. Professional ethical conduct guided by deontological theory is defined in terms of moral duties, rights and contracts, which are viewed as general, universal or universalisable rules or prescriptions. Emphasis is on delivering universally impartial regard for the professionally relevant needs of others (Carr, 2005). Moral education should provide students with an understanding of what moral principles are, as well as rules that guide the application of those principles. To achieve this understanding teachers should challenge students' moral understanding and sensitise them to moral issues by creating cognitive dissonance through debate, dilemmas and questions (Kohlberg, 1981). This approach presumes that anyone with the capacity for reason can come to act in a moral way through moral training; that it is possible to design tests to decide if moral principles have been learned; and that this will have an effect on how people actually behave. Either it presumes moral character, which people bring to the training is less important than the training, or that moral character can be developed through training.

This theory has been criticised for its emphasis on moral knowledge and understanding, rather than moral action. An alternative view is much more particularistic and individualistic. It emphasises virtues or moral character. It also emphasises that becoming a good person, that moral character, is not merely about achieving mature moral reasoning capacities. According to Flanagan (1991, 1996) in real life we do not operate through a series of moral dilemmas, which require a judgement of the right solution to each case. We must act in real time when there is no time for considered reflection as presumed in the deontological approach. Moral education in this view concerns cultivating good character, understood as having "virtuous dispositions to perceive, think, feel and act in appropriate ways in appropriate situations" (Jones, 2005: 143). Moral education is "primarily a process of learning how: how to recognize a wide variety of complex situations and how to respond to them appropriately" (Flanagan, 1996: 124). According to this approach, formal moral education as part of professional training is not likely to be effective. Character is presumed to be largely established from a young age. Habits of reflection, empathy, care compassion, fairness acquired in childhood and early schooling are likely to shape receptiveness to formal moral education later in life.[19]

We adopt a middle-way approach that recognises important aspects of both philosophical theories. It is important to recognise the importance of exercising ethical judgements in situations as near as possible to real life situations, but under the guidance of peers and mentors. We would emphasise viewing a profession as a community of practitioners that develops, maintains and supports its own norms of behaviour and articulates ethical principles in a variety of ways. Far more than formal documents such as codes and guidance notes, and more than ensuring that professional ethics is covered in initial professional qualifications and in continuing professional development, professional associations need to be actively promoting discussion and debate about issues that underlie ethical competence, by encouraging members to write about ethical issues in their magazines and journals,

---

[19] There is a parallel here between Schön's emphasis on knowing-in-action and reflection-in-action as key to professional technical competence and the virtue ethics position, as opposed to critiques of Schön, which emphasise reflection before and after action as being important and the deontological approach, see Chapter 4.

but encouraging debate on these issues at branch/regional level, by encouraging the formation of special interest groups on different aspects of ethical behaviour, by supporting research into ethical competence. We would emphasise that the debate as to whether one can teach character can be misleading. It encourages an either/or attitude towards supporting ethical competence, whereas what we believe is likely to be most important is creating a climate of opinion and a culture of practice that supports ethical competence from a variety of sources. It is the combination of supports and activities that is important.

Providing an Ethical Code and a few lectures on it is not enough to instil ethical competence. Educating for ethical competence will generally only be achieved through initial work within the profession, possibly as part of formal residency, articles of other forms of apprenticeship schemes as well as being part of a professional community throughout the working life of the professional. This point has been made clearly by Flanagan:

> ... moral responsiveness does not (normally) involve deployment of a set of special-purpose rules or algorithms that are individually applied to all, and only, the problems for which they are designed specifically. Nor does moral responsiveness normally involve deployment of single general-purpose rule or algorithm (...) designed to deal with each and every moral problem. Moral issues are heterogeneous in kind, and the moral community wisely trains us to possess a vast array of moral competencies suited – often in complex combinations and configurations – to multifarious domains.
> (1996: 127)

6.3 Education provision on ethics as part of initial professional qualifications

According to the 2006 PARN Professionalisation of Professional Associations Survey, 61% of UK professional associations and 78% of Irish associations include courses on ethics in their initial professional qualifications (IPQ). As can be seen from Table 6:1, this was in fact the most commonly included subject content of IPQ from among the six categories offered in the questionnaire (other than profession specific requirements) in both countries.

Table 6:1 Initial professional qualifications: 2006 surveys

Content of initial professional qualifications	UK	Ireland
Profession specific requirements	96%	100%
Generic management skills	49%	67%
Ethics	61%	78%
Interprofessional team working	43%	61%
Client service	42%	50%
IT	26%	50%
International practice	14%	17%
Other	8%	22%
Sample size	92	18

Health and safety, environment and communications were included in the 'other' category as well as examples of complications in the way initial professional qualifications are delivered.

The proportion offering ethics as a special subject in initial professional qualifications was exactly the same in both UK and Irish samples of respondents that answered this question in both 2003 and 2006. It is somewhat disappointing that there has not been an increase in emphasis on ethics education as part of initial professional qualifications in either country during this 3-year period, at least according to the evidence from our surveys.

6.4 Continuing professional development

Continuing professional development (CPD) is of particular interest in relation to ethical competence. CPD is a contributor to the development of professional competence in general and a range of competencies in particular including ethical competency. However it can also be, as noted in Chapter 5, an explicit item of obligation in Ethical Codes (both maintaining one's own CPD and even supporting the CPD of others). That is, for some professional associations CPD can also be a criterion by which ethical competence is judged, to carry out CPD, whether the content of CPD is ethical competency or not, is regarded as an element in the achievement of ethical competence because it is referred to in the Ethical Code.

6.4.1   CPD as a method of maintaining competence

There has been a sea change in attitudes towards education and training of professionals. The fundamental change has been a growing acceptance that initial professional qualifications are not enough and cannot be treated by professional associations as the end of the period of education and training of professionals. Professionals must actively keep up their knowledge of the field and their repertoire of techniques. They must in particular be aware of new techniques available and of the latest thinking about the efficacy of the techniques they use in daily practice. They must continually develop themselves as professionals. This has always been understood informally. The formation of professional associations has usually been stimulated by individuals in service occupations who wish to share their understanding of the latest techniques through organised activities: lectures and social and training events organised by the association; newsletters and journals; and through branch and special interest group activities. It has always been assumed that professionals would regularly read these materials and participate in activities organised by their associations. In early years of an association, when the membership is small and closely associated with the organisation of association activities, this can be a reasonable assumption.

What has changed is the formalisation of expectations for members of professional associations to carry out their professional development in a manner that is in accord with a stated policy of the professional association; that is, to follow a programme of CPD activities and events, which are either designed by the professional association or accredited in some way by them (see Friedman et al., 2000 Chapter 2 for a history of CPD in the UK). All of what 'counts' as CPD need not be formal training or specific events. It can include reading journals and other activities. However, what makes it CPD is that it is included in the remit of what the professional association considers to be CPD for that profession. What is new is that professional associations now provide organised support for their members' CPD: guidelines and other supports such as mentoring schemes, reflection materials and standardised recording methods, as well as advice.

There is confusion in many people's minds concerning the degree of compulsion professional associations impose upon their members for fulfilling their CPD expectations. Three different terms are in common use: voluntary, obligatory and compulsory. In general voluntary and compulsory policies are straightforward. Compulsory policies are monitored and sanctions are imposed if CPD requirements are not fulfilled. Voluntary policies may be monitored, but there is no sanction if CPD is not undertaken. What is offered is left to the professional to decide how much to partake in and whether they pursue any of the opportunities developed or made available by their professional association. As noted in a previous PARN publication, this association between compulsion and sanctions is not always consistently followed by associations (see Friedman et al., 2000, Chapter 6), some do not impose sanctions for non-compliance, but claim that their CPD policies are compulsory or mandatory, a few impose sanctions while declaring their policy to be voluntary.

Surprisingly, from the perspective of ethical competence, obligatory CPD policies are less well understood and appear to be declining. Obligatory CPD policies are those that are required in the same way as other obligations that might appear in the Ethical Code. Sometimes, as noted earlier, the obligation to carry out CPD is explicitly stated in the code, though often more general terms are used, such as the obligation to maintain one's competence or to keep up-to-date.

According to the 2006 PARN Professionalisation of Professional Associations Survey 85% of the 110 respondents in the UK and 67% of the 21 Irish respondents had a CPD policy. The distributions of those policies based on the compliance requirements are shown in Table 6:2.

Table 6:2 CPD compliance policies: 2006 surveys

CPD compliance policy	UK	Ireland
Compulsory	21%	43%
Obligatory	21%	7%
Voluntary	44%	36%
Mixed	14%	14%
Sample size	91	14

The mixed cases are generally ones that are compulsory for specific member categories; chartered, technician, fellows and only voluntary for others. Sometimes mixed refers to only professional members for whom it is obligatory or compulsory, and only voluntary for affiliate members. A few have CPD as compulsory for new members only.

Table 6:3 CPD compliance policies: matched samples 2003 vs 2006

	UK		Ireland	
CPD compliance policy	2003	2006	2003	2006
Compulsory	14%	18%	44%	55%
Obligatory	34%	26%	22%	11%
Voluntary	36%	40%	33%	22%
Mixed	16%	16%	0	11%
Sample size	50	50	9	9

There were relatively few who responded to this question in both surveys, particularly in Ireland, however, it seems clear from Table 6:3 that in both countries the proportion of obligatory policies has fallen and compulsory programmes has grown. However the proportions changing on average are not great.

It seems that CPD is considered to be so important by a substantial and growing proportion of professional associations, particularly in Ireland, that they feel the process of monitoring and imposing sanctions on their members should be different, more strict, than that which applies to other obligations specified in their codes of conduct. This is possibly because CPD requirements can be made very clear and simple to understand and therefore it is relatively straightforward to gauge if they are not being adhered to. It is much more difficult to sanction a member for not acting fairly or showing respect for the dignity of clients or patients when there is a large grey area between obvious unfairness and lack of respect on one hand and the accepted lack of consideration that is part of the way busy people must operate, particularly associated with bureaucratic organisations. The amount of time that clients or patients receive and the degree of politeness shown may not always be what it could be, but this can hardly lead to someone being thrown out of a professional association or losing their status as a fellow or a chartered member. It would also be considered too much of an imposition on practice to monitor this closely. It is different with CPD. Not fulfilling CPD requirements, though also subject to some grey areas due to possible differences in interpretation of what counts as CPD, is nevertheless, much clearer. It is easier to monitor and therefore easier to impose sanctions for non-compliance.

Of those 91 UK respondents to the 2006 survey with a CPD policy, 70% stated that they have a monitoring system for determining whether members are participating in CPD. The Irish equivalent proportion was comparable, 64% of the 14 that had a CPD policy. Of the 64 that monitored CPD of their members in the UK, the following methods were used:

- Questionnaires sent to all members, but no compulsion to reply, 9%

- Random voluntary audit of a sample of members' CPD records, 31%

- Random compulsory audit of a sample of members' CPD records, 25%

- Compulsory audit of all members' CPD records, 14%

- Other, 20%.

Participation in CPD can be evidenced in different ways, some fairly simple, a record of activities, but others, more substantial for what may be regarded as professional competence. That is, evidence of planning and evidence of reflection is required. Table 6:4 provides the responses to this question comparing UK and Irish responses.

Table 6:4 Methods of gathering evidence of CPD participation, 2006

Method of gathering evidence on CPD	UK	Ireland
Record of activities	88%	86%
Evidence of planning	47%	36%
Evidence of reflection	39%	29%
No evidence	11%	7%
Sample size	92	14

The manner of CPD monitoring has been changing. Early systems were primarily based on inputs, that is, simply recording hours spent on CPD or 'points' based on hours and the nature of the activities. More recently professional associations have been moving towards output-based systems of monitoring CPD. Ultimately the criterion ought to be evidence for how actual practice has developed, or improved, due to participation in CPD. Ultimately this would require peer review of practice before and after CPD activities. There are other ways of monitoring CPD that, while not providing definitive evidence of improved practice, are likely to be correlated with improved practice. Evidence of planning and particularly evidence of reflection associated with CPD activities are two ways this may be achieved. As can be seen from Table 6:4, a fairly substantial proportion of associations in the UK do gather evidence of reflection and almost half gather evidence of planning. The proportions of Irish associations are lower for both. However, in both countries monitoring through gathering evidence of planning and reflection is growing as can be seen from Table 6:5.

Table 6:5   Methods of gathering evidence on CPD: matched samples 2003 vs 2006

	UK		Ireland	
Method of gathering evidence on CPD	**2003**	**2006**	**2003**	**2006**
Record of activities	88%	92%	88%	88%
Evidence of planning	42%	56%	22%	33%
Evidence of reflection	37%	40%	0	22%
No evidence	12%	8%	0	0
Sample size	52	52	9	9

As noted in Chapter 4 both technical and ethical competence requires, in addition to knowledge and the right attitudes, for practitioners to be able to act in a professional manner in the heat of the moment, at the point of practice. This requires the exercise of reflective practice in all forms discussed in that chapter, knowing-in-action, reflecting-in-action as well as reflecting before and after practice. Arguably the habit of reflection in its many forms can be encouraged by practice. Reflecting on CPD activities is an important opportunity to develop this habit of reflection. In this sense CPD can contribute not only to professional competencies, but also to professional competence. It is not only the particular subjects of CPD that are important for increasing the repertoire of technical and ethical competencies professionals can acquire, but also CPD, if it is organised in a 'professional' manner by practitioners (supported by their association) can contribute to technical and ethical competence of professionals.

6.4.2 CPD and ethical training

The most obvious connection between CPD and ethical competence is for CPD to include activities or courses explicitly concerned with the Ethical Code and other subjects associated with professional ethics.

As noted in Chapter 5, according to the 2006 PARN Professionalisation of Professional Associations Survey, 22% of professional associations in the UK and 40% in Ireland include courses or seminars on ethics other than initial qualifications (Table 5:1). Again as with including ethics as a special subject in initial professional qualifications, the proportions offering courses or seminars on ethics other than initial qualifications was exactly the same in both UK and Irish samples of respondents that answered this question in both 2003 and 2006 (Tables 5:2 and 5:3).

6.5 Case study on education and ethical competence: ICAEW

Overall we believe, as noted in the previous chapter, that the accounting associations in the UK are particularly active in supporting the ethical competence of their members. In the following case study a wide range of activities undertaken by the Institute of Chartered Accountants in England and Wales (ICAEW) concerning support for ethics in both initial professional qualifications and continuing professional development. Their approach to disciplinary procedures is also interesting.

Case study 6.1
Anne Davis- Ethics Manager, The Institute of Chartered Accountants in England and Wales.

The Institute of Chartered Accountants in England and Wales (ICAEW) offers an extremely wide variety of ethical education, guidance and support for its members. Within the ICAEW, ethics is incorporated within the following areas:

- The Ethical Code

- Education- including the initial professional qualification and compulsory structured training in ethics and work-based learning programmes

- Continuing Professional Development (CPD)

- Member support- including help lines and help sheets.

- Enforcement- the disciplinary procedure

- Thought leadership

Ethical education
Ethics is incorporated into the Associate Chartered Accountant (ACA) qualification at all stages. The ICAEW is in the process of reviewing the syllabus and the changes will come into effect in September 2007 when ethics will comprise 20% of the syllabus and be integrated into 11 out of the 15 modules. However, none of these modules are entirely dedicated to ethics. For example within the Audit and Assurance module there is discussion of the ICAEW's Code of Ethics, along with IFAC's and the Auditing Practice Board's ethical standards. As Anne Davis, the Ethics Manager, commented:

> *The ICAEW is of the view that an integrated approach is the best way of teaching ethics rather than stand-alone ethics module within the exam. Ethics is incorporated into the initial professional qualification, work-based learning and structured training on ethics programmes. This will ensure that students are always realistically examined on ethical matters within a broader context.*

The decision to increase the prominence of ethics in their initial qualification is due to the increasing importance and sophistication of professional judgement matters and requests from firms for students with not only high technical competencies but also high ethical competencies.

The ACA qualification is supported by the ICAEW's compulsory work-based learning and structured training in ethics programmes, which students undertake before qualifying. These have a big ethical component in them. For example, students are given ethical case study type discussion questions to work through with their trainer. Both of these programmes are being updated and enhanced by new and more sophisticated versions in September 2007. The new structured training in ethics programme will take a wider approach than just professional ethics including relevant ethical questions from a wider societal context. There will be a new web-based training package split into three stages, and students will have to pass the end of stage activities in order to qualify. The first stage is to gain a general knowledge of ethics, the second to work through relatively black and white case studies and the third deals with more complicated case studies in order to develop professional judgement. Each individual will have a named counsellor within their organisation to provide ethical and general advice, who will carry out six-monthly reviews during this programme.

CPD

The ICAEW has had a CPD scheme for members for over 25 years. The current, outputs-based, scheme which is mandatory for all members, has been in place since January 2005. It is centred on the motto and four stage approach "Reflect, Act, Impact and Declare", rather than taking a focus on the number of CPD points, "The ICAEW was of the view that there was a need to make CPD more relevant to members and make them think about what they needed in order to do their job ethically and competently."

The 'stages' method follows the process of firstly reflecting on what is expected and which areas of the role need improvement, secondly acting by exercising professional judgement in deciding what type and how much CPD to do and thirdly evaluating how successful it was and whether targets set have been met and fourthly making an annual declaration of compliance to the ICAEW. The ICAEW emphasises that courses and conferences are by no means the only things that comprise CPD. Examples of other possible activities include technical reading, use of the Internet and e-learning, workshops with peers, and meetings with experts. Individuals are expected to keep a record of their CPD and to make a declaration at the end of the year. Every year a large sample of members are selected to provide evidence of what CPD they have undertaken. The reviewer will consider whether or not what is being done is appropriate to the role and whether it has enabled the member to exercise professional ethics.

There is a members-only access CPD website within the ICAEW's main website which includes an ethical guide. This has interactive ethical dilemmas to work through online which give possible outcomes: "It illustrates that in many cases there are no right or wrong answers, it's applying ethical principles and exercising professional judgement."

The website also includes reference guides covering topics such as the Ethical Code, bribery and corruption, and whistle-blowing.

Disciplinary procedures
The ICAEW have a formalised complaints and disciplinary procedure. Any complaints received from members of the public will go through to an assessment process, and unless there is no basis for the complaint, will then continue on to investigation and where appropriate discipline. Complaints are considered not only in terms of ethics, but also in terms of whether the situation could be seen as "bringing discredit to the profession", part of the code. Punishments include fines, expulsion and withdrawal from audit registration. The names of offenders and a short paragraph about the event and what the sanction was are published in the back of the accounting magazine. Anne sees these publications as having both a negative and positive effect on how the ICAEW is viewed by the public:

> But, if we didn't have a disciplinary process in place to ensure and be seen to ensure that members of the public had some recourse in the case of unacceptable action by members, that would be seen as a negative.

Public interest cases are dealt with by the Accounting Investigations and Disciplinary Board, a separate body which is part of the independent Financial Reporting Council.

6.6   Methods for teaching character

According to Puka (1999: 131) there are six distinct methods that have been used in character education programmes:

- Basic values and virtues instruction

- Establishing and enforcing codes of conduct

- Telling stories with moral lessons

- Modelling desirable traits and values

- Identifying moral exemplars and their traits from history, literature and religion

- Outreach opportunities in the form of service projects that allow students to exercise good traits and values

These are methods that can and should be used in professional education and CPD for all professions. One particular method that we consider to be interesting is the use of moral dilemmas to illustrate situations professionals are likely to encounter and to help sensitise them to when they are in a situation that requires careful reflection on ethical consequences of their actions.

6.7 Moral dilemmas: a technique for educating practitioners in ethical competence

6.7.1 Introduction

Ethical conduct can be supported by case studies of moral dilemmas. A moral dilemma may be described as a situation in which three conditions apply; that is, someone is:

- Required to do each of two or more actions

- Able to do each of them

- Not able do both or all of them during the time period under consideration.

Here are a few well known examples.

In the novel *Sophie's Choice* (Styron, 1980) Sophie is interred in a Nazi concentration camp with her two children. A guard tells her that one child will live and one will be killed, but Sophie must decide which will be killed. Furthermore, if she refuses to choose, both will be killed. In this case she has a symmetrical obligation to each child.

Most moral dilemmas involve asymmetrical obligations in that the different actions involve obligations of different kinds. For example

Sartre (1957) describes a student who wants to avenge his brother's death by the Germans in 1940 and to fight what he regards to be evil. He is living with his mother and was her sole consolation in life. The student is torn between personal devotion to his mother (of limited scope but certain level of contribution to value) and attempting to contribute to the defeat of an aggressor (of wide scope, but uncertain level of contribution to value).

Professionals often face such dilemmas such as the physician who must decide whether to withdraw life support from a dying patient. Physicians may believe that their obligation is to prolong life. They may also believe that unpreventable pain should not be tolerated in patients. Criminal lawyers defending a client have an obligation of confidentiality towards client disclosures, but also an obligation to candour before the court which requires them to inform the court when their client commits perjury. (See Freedman, 1975).

The 'solution' to the moral dilemma comes when one decides on the degree of obligation implied by the first condition. This implies that there is a hierarchy of obligations. Philosophers have argued that even if there were a hierarchy of obligations in people's minds at any one time and for any one person, it is unlikely that this hierarchy would be both invariant over time and consistent between people in different circumstances. The more complete and detailed an ordering may be, the less likely that it will apply in all circumstances, the less likely it will be that all circumstances in which it should apply can be sufficiently described in detail.

Therefore much of what appears to be a moral dilemma or many moral dilemmas at any moment in time for any specific person can be 'solved' by further information. For example, a dilemma may be perceived because a person mistakenly thinks all three of these conditions apply, whereas they do not all apply, or they are uncertain as to whether the conditions apply. Clearly here further investigation is possible and can be enlightening. Thus the facts may be uncertain and can be clarified.

Second the consequences may be an issue. For example the consequences of each action will affect the level of obligation to each action. It may be that the hierarchy of obligations depends on the consequences of not fulfilling an obligation. What precisely are the consequences of fulfilling or not fulfilling a particular obligation may be in doubt.

A third problem may be that particular actions may not be clearly connected to particular obligations.

A somewhat different problem of consequences of one's acts affecting the nature of the dilemma and it's poignancy is the emotional consequences of the obligation not fulfilled. In the *Sophie's Choice* situation, the child not saved will cause guilt and remorse even if it is clear to Sophie that she can in fact only save one of her children if she chooses to condemn one of them. There seems to be a clear moral dilemma here. The proper solution is to save one of the children, even if there is no basis on which to choose which one. Whatever she does, a child of hers will die and she will feel remorse, even if realistically it was the best she could do in the circumstances.

It may be that there is a clear moral hierarchy between the two obligations. Here too there can be remorse for the obligation not fulfilled. We need to distinguish regret from remorse. Regret is broader and is a bad feeling over the occurrence of a situation that does not require the agent to believe that they have done anything wrong. A teacher may regret having to punish a pupil for misbehaviour even when the action is morally required. Even wider, one may feel regret for situations which one has no causal connection with, such as a neighbour being robbed or a war in a distant country. In this sense the extent of remorse and the extent of regret are variables. The differential in level of obligation between the one fulfilled versus the necessary obligation unfulfilled, may affect the level of remorse, but not the level of regret. The level of regret will be more affected by the dire consequences of not fulfilling the lesser obligation rather than the obligation gap that justifies not fulfilling that obligation. The gap between them may be characterised as a cognitive component that is added to the experiential component with remorse or guilt. This is the belief that one has done something wrong and takes responsibility for the act.

6.7.2   Context for the use of moral dilemmas

Ethical sensitivity of students can be particularly supported if they attempt to deal with cases of moral dilemmas through role-play as well as individual study, especially if role-play is facilitated by someone who understands not only the code, but also someone who has experienced actual dilemmas in practice (someone with both a specific ethical competency and general ethical competence). Many professions use practitioners to provide tuition on the professional in society or professional ethics. There is a danger here, however, when this occurs within a higher education context. That is, academics that normally teach students, may not be sufficiently familiar with real life moral dilemmas (they may only have an ethical competency) and so practitioners are called in to provide the element of 'realism'. Unfortunately, in academic courses aimed primarily at technical knowledge and particularly at theoretical underpinnings of such knowledge and at fostering a critical attitude towards that knowledge, there can be a prejudice against 'straightforward' practitioners who come in an speak from experience rather than a theoretical or critical perspective. The cultural line between academic and practitioner can spread to the students.

The use of moral dilemmas as a pedagogic tool can be practiced at any level of training, however many are best associated with CPD in that they will have greatest impact if the professional can recognise the situation from experience.

The expressed objectives in studying a case study of a moral dilemma in a CPD situation can be summarised as 4 steps.

- Recognise the ethical issues when they arise

- Know where to go in the guidelines for guidance on what action to take

- Apply guidelines appropriately within the case study

- Transfer what you have learned to your own work situation.

6.8　Case studies on cases of ethical dilemmas: SII, IMC

The following case study emphasises how important case studies of ethical dilemmas are for developing ethical competence beyond mere knowledge of the letter of codes of conduct.

Case study 6.2
Based on an interview with Simon Culhane - Chief Executive Officer, The Securities and Investment Institute

The Securities and Investment Institute (SII) reviewed and updated their professional code for the second time in its history in 2006, after it was seen as necessary to give trust and integrity greater prominence within the Institute. Simon Culhane, CEO, sees the code as important in order to help members attain and maintain competence:

> *In some cases it's more than maintaining, it's actually creating the culture. You're moving essentially from having just the qualification which is fairly technical, to learning how to behave in the right environment and apply those skills.*

In accordance with this, the SII produced an ethics module in their CPD scheme in 2006. They have also produced a book of case studies, which will be sent to all members in about two months time. In the meantime, a series of ethical dilemmas under the title 'grey matters' (because the answer is not black or white) are on the website. Some are generic ethical situations that have been produced by senior level practitioners, drawing from their everyday experience. Having real life examples helps members relate to the scenarios and apply the learning to their own experiences. "The concept of the case study is to tease out what is right, 'the spirit', rather than what the rules are, 'the letter'."

One example of these case studies is the issue of tickets to World Cup football matches and when this crosses the line between acceptable corporate hospitality into bribery. In this scenario, the advice given was to consider if the gift was outside the normal lifestyle of the recipient. If it was, then there may be an obligation created and the gift should be refused. Another example considers the actions to be taken on the discovery that one of the star performers within a company is HIV positive. While these are set within a financial context they are generic issues and can be applied to many other professional associations.

In addition to this the SII have a whistle-blowing telephone line and an email address run by practitioner members for situations when all internal sources have been exhausted.

Simon's belief is that integrity and ethics are very much a part of the UK culture, with currently much scope for exportation abroad. The

SII's partners around the globe are very interested in their professional code and some use it as a basis for their own, particularly regarding corporate governance standards: "corporate governance is very close to behaviour of openness and transparency, which is the fundamental element behind many codes of conduct."

Case study 6.3
Based on an interview with Sabrina Ahmed - Professional Standards Manager, The Institute of Business Consulting

The Institute of Business Consulting (IBC) has a set of ethical guidelines that predates 2004 and it has not been revised since its formulation. The IBC have recently commenced a review programme looking at these ethical guidelines to see what kind of support services and products they can provide for members. This was prompted by a brief audit undertaken in May 2006 when Sabrina Ahmed, the Professional Standards Manager joined the organisation. A review steering group has been formed to manage the review, in order to represent members from various sectors. They intend to analyse the professional development and standards offering, including their code of practice and ethical guidelines to determine how fit for purpose they are, and use techniques such as benchmarking, stakeholder analysis, as well as PARN resources to see how they fit into the market and meet the needs of members and the general public.

Currently most of the ethical support for members is based on the availability of human resources. If a member had an ethical dilemma they would go directly to Sabrina for guidance. There is no specific helpline or specific ethical guidance available to members apart from a set of questions for possible ethical dilemmas. These are guidelines for individual members to consider and proceed at their own discretion. They are based around three sections:

• Background - in order to help place the dilemma in context, and objectively establish all the facts

• Vulnerabilities - in order to help understand where vulnerabilities lie and to formulate a solution

• Transparency - in order to establish whether or not the issue is transparent from all angles and the reasons behind this

These types of guidelines are particularly important for management consultants considering the nature of their work. Some are independent and will go into external organisations where they are less likely to have the same kind of ethical support from colleagues or a parent organisation as others. Regarding ethical support, Sabrina commented: "As far as prompting the review, it is valid having questions, but there needs to be more behind that to provide a better ethics support provision for members."

- Chapter 7 -
Remedial supports: complaints and disciplinary procedures

7.1   Introduction

Complaints and disciplinary procedures can support ethical competence in a number of ways. They are intended to:

- Rid the profession of incompetents, thereby preserving the ethical competence of a profession as a whole

- Reassure the public that complaints against members of the profession will be taken seriously

- Deter behaviour which is beneath the standards of ethical competence as set out in professional Ethical Codes both by clarifying what are serious breaches of ethical competence and assuring members of the profession that the professional body will take such breaches seriously.

Together, if these objects are achieved, complaints and disciplinary procedures can be a fundamental bulwark of professionalism. In the minds of the public, these are arguably the most important ways of demonstrating that professions are serious about their ethical competence as a community of practitioners. However, in the past many professional bodies have acted as though they consider that publicity concerning how they have dealt with members of the profession who have not been performing up to expected standards would harm the image of the profession as a whole. Because all their members are expected to be both technically and ethically competent, those concerned with complaints and discipline have acted as though they have had an overriding concern that the trust the public hold for that profession would be dented by publicizing these cases. Also many professional bodies have taken more of a remedial than a punitive view of professionals who have transgressed. While this is helpful and in many instances will enhance the public good, there is a concern that such a view is more motivated by self-protection than the greater good as the blame culture has taken more of a hold. Not publicising that punishments are meted out and not explaining more publicly the rationale for the decisions that are taken has, arguably, damaged trust in the process of professional self regulation far more than greater revelation of these regulatory procedures would have done.

Complaints and disciplinary procedures can have a negative effect on public opinion of particular professions if they come to be perceived as purely symbolic activities that have no bite. The value of complaints and disciplinary procedures to reassure the public depends on public perception of how fair and timely the procedures are which link complaints to discipline or other remedial action taken by the professional body or the professionals complained against. Punitive action by the professional body may not be warranted or necessary, in some cases a simple apology or recourse to alternative disputes resolution procedures (mediation in particular) will suffice, again as long as such actions are taken in a timely and sensitive manner. However, it is necessary to take severe action against those that are clearly not up to the standards of technical and ethical competence as defined by CPD policies and the Ethical Code.

Formal mechanisms for dealing with complaints against members of a profession are relatively new and they are generally becoming more formal and more substantive, more 'professional'. For example, more professional bodies that are concerned with regulation are involving lay people in their procedures. We suspect that more professions are using more public punishments such as 'naming and shaming' those who have been found wanting as well as generally publishing their findings. It is also likely that more of these procedures themselves will come to be open to the public. These changes reflect the same pressures on professions that have led to codes being revised and made more accessible in recent years as was discussed in Chapter 5. They may be considered responses to direct government concern about mechanisms for dealing with complaints, and indirectly this process of professionalisation is fuelled by the change in attitude towards professionals in general, that is, that considered or 'earned' trust has replaced 'blind trust' in professionals.

7.2 Extent and nature of complaints and disciplinary procedures

The PARN Professionalisation of Professional Associations Survey of 2006, found that 74% of respondents responded positively to the question "In the event of a complaint against a member, do you have a formalised disciplinary procedure?"

Respondents were then asked whether this procedure included any of the activities listed in Table 7:1. The percentages reported are of the whole sample of 110 respondents in the UK and 21 in Ireland. Of the UK sample, 73% responded positively, as did 62% of the Irish sample. For those that responded positively, Table 7:1 shows what this involves.

Table 7:1 Activities associated with disciplinary procedures: 2006 surveys

Disciplinary activities involving;	UK	Ireland
Right of appeal	83%	85%
Penalties from a range of options	80%	77%
Participation of lay people	43%	39%
Publication of findings	29%	31%
Other	4%	8%
Sample size	80	13

Only 3 ticked 'other' among UK respondents. One of these stated that they hold public hearings. One stated that the penalty was removal from the Society. For one the disciplinary procedures are in the process of being established. The one that ticked 'other' in Ireland stated that findings may be publicised if warranted, but this is not automatic.

The proportions of associations reporting this range of disciplinary activities are remarkably similar between the two countries. Publication of findings is reported by just under a third of associations that have a formalised disciplinary procedure. We would regard this as rather low and look forward to it increasing in future.

We believe that the inclusion of lay people in disciplinary procedures is a relatively new and positive development in terms of assuring the public that their interests will be preserved in these proceedings. This is not a guarantee of impartiality, but it can help. PARN is developing a clearing house for individuals with experience in one professional association to volunteer to be lay representatives in disciplinary or governance arrangements in other professional associations.

7.3 The dilemma of disciplinary procedures for certain professions

Potential severity of the consequences of disciplinary action taken by a professional association depends critically on the legal and market status of membership of that professional association. Some professions are licensed by statute, and individuals must belong to the professional association in order to practice the profession. In this case suspension or exclusion from membership in effect involves the loss of livelihood in an activity that is likely to have taken many years of education and experience to acquire. Other professions are not licensed, but membership of certain professional associations represent a clear signal to the market for services and employment that those who are members of that professional association, and have the relevant post-nominals, are 'better' than others offering the same or related services or technical competencies. In the UK, and less so in Ireland, such professional associations can be Chartered, though the degree of market power represented by Chartered status varies considerably among professions. Loss of statutory licence would result in loss of livelihood, and the Human Rights Act is implicated by the disciplinary procedures of these professions. Loss of chartered status would not automatically result in loss of the ability to practice, but would make practice more difficult. The dilemma of disciplinary procedures for such associations will be the cost involved in prosecuting cases that involve the Human Rights Act. Those being disciplined have a right to a trial-like procedure which takes time and resources to carry out.

For other professions there is the dilemma of discipline. That is, there are no punishments that the association can impose that can act as a deterrent because the ultimate punishment, removal from the association's register will have little material effect on the offender.

Even the less substantial punishments, such as fines, are difficult to enforce if individuals can avoid them by simply relinquishing their membership of the professional association.

7.4 The problem of limited effective punishments

Traditionally the disciplinary procedures of professional associations have been designed to determine fitness to practice of individual members. The basic punishment for misconduct is to be removed from the register either permanently (exclusion) or for a period of time after which the individual can reapply for admission (suspension). In the latter case there may be conditions attached, such as a demonstration that appropriate training or medical treatment has been undertaken, or that he or she has established certain procedures to help prevent recurrence of the offence.

Another category of punishments is reprimands, admonishments, warnings and advice. A reprimand is usually intended to be punitive and kept on a member's records. It may or may not be published. Admonishments are not usually kept on file and tend to be similar to a warning. Often professional associations give rehabilitation guidance to manage the risk of the offence re-occurring. Some professional associations use the term warning, which again can be accompanied by guidance to prevent recurrence. Finally some issue advice to members who may be in danger of crossing the line of misconduct.

A third category of punishments is financial (fines or awarding costs). Many professional associations that include fines and costs among their sanctions have never applied them because they are unable to enforce payment without going to court. Some professional associations will award costs at every stage of their procedure. It is rare at the investigatory stage, more usual at the disciplinary hearing stage, and almost always on appeal.

Finally, an interesting punishment is to downgrade the membership category of a complainant or remove some privilege or status level such as fellowship status. This has the advantage of not being so severe as to involve the loss of livelihood. It is also within the control of the association, it does not require money to be recovered.

Table 7:2 shows the different proportions of respondents using different punishments based on their disciplinary procedures according to the 2006 PARN survey for the UK and Ireland. Respondents were first asked if their disciplinary procedure involves a range of penalty options, and then were offered the list shown in Table 7:2 to indicate which of them applied.

Table 7:2 Punishments as a result of disciplinary procedures: 2006

Disciplinary procedures: punishments	UK	Ireland
Permanent striking off (expulsion)	88%	100%
Temporary striking off (suspension)	77%	90%
Removal of some privileges or status level (e.g. fellowship)	42%	30%
Proof of competence required (re-examination)	22%	20%
Fine paid to your organisation	22%	40%
Fine paid to those offended against	6%	20%
Name and shame	48%	60%
A quiet word or warning	61%	90%
Public apology required	16%	10%
Other	11%	20%
Sample size	64	10

The most common punishments are expulsion, suspension and warnings. These were the only ones that were penalty options for more than half of those responding to this question in the UK. In Ireland the proportions using these three punishments were even higher at 90% or 100%. These are the traditional punishments in our opinion. Newer punishments fall into three categories, public forms of disgrace, fines and removal of privileges.

Name and shame is a relatively common form of punishment, being available to almost half the sample in the UK and 60% in Ireland. However we suspect that there is a wide range of publicity given to the naming. For most naming will occur in sources that would only be read by members of the profession, nevertheless this can be effective as a deterrent to others for those who wish to remain in the profession after disciplinary procedures and as long as it does not apply to too many in the profession.

Fines are not commonly used in the UK, but rather more common in Ireland. As noted above, fines can be difficult to collect if members decide not to renew their membership of the association, which they can easily do if the profession is not statutorily regulated. Fines paid to those offended against are rare.

Perhaps the most interesting penalty is the removal of privileges in the sense that this is a punishment that is well within the power of the professional association to impose, it is well within the limits of being one the one hand, not overly drastic as expulsion or suspension would be in terms of the Human Rights Act, that is, removing one's means of employment, and on the other hand, much more serious and seen to be serious, compared with a quiet word or a warning. It may also be more serious in the public's eye than naming and shaming. The strength of this punishment within this range, is largely dependent on the ability of the professional body to create internal status or privilege levels. This can be problematic. There is a tension between the notion of equal treatment for all who are part of the profession and the creation of incentives and rewards for distinguished behaviour in practice, or in other means of increasing the reputation of the profession.

Interestingly the proportion that allow for fines to be paid to those offended against and public apologies required were the two least frequently used punishments. There may well be room here for the concept of public redress to be expanded in future.

7.4.1   Case study: GDC

Case study 7.1
Based on documentation from the UK General Dental Council.

The UK General Dental Council (GDC) recently introduced the Dental Complaints Service (DCS) and a new set of Fitness to Practice Committees in July 2006. The DCS is meant to resolve complaints about private dental treatment where no concerns about impairment of fitness to practise are apparent. It is instructive to see the issues which come to the DSC which should be referred to the GDC under fitness to practice procedures. These are:

- Any criminal charge or conviction

- Lack of adequate indemnity arrangements

- Violence

- Dishonesty

- Inadequate infection control

- General anaesthetic or conscious sedation offered or performed in breach of GDC guidance

- Abuse of the dentist/patient relationship

- Misuse of drugs or alcohol, or other health impairment not apparently under effective control

- Practising contrary to medical advice

- Self prescription of prescription drugs or other abuse of prescription rights

- Recklessness as to consent

- Breach of patient confidentiality

- Seriously negligent care or treatment

- Illegal unregistered practice

- A dental professional's involvement in any serious adverse incident involving death or serious lasting harm.

This is not an exhaustive list. DCS may refer a case to the GDC at any time and at that time DCS involvement in the case ends. DCS will not undertake complaints resolution in parallel with consideration by GDC and vice versa, if the DCS is dealing with a complaint, the GDC will not undertake a parallel investigation. It is also possible for Professional Standards Department Staff to refer a case to the DCS and if so will do this at the earliest opportunity and will advise complainants and enquirers accordingly.

7.5   Complaints procedures

According to guidelines published by The Cabinet Office (1998) to assist public sector organisations improve their complaints systems, a complaints systems should be:

- Easy to *access* and well publicised

- *Speedy* – with fixed time limits for action and keeping people informed of progress

- *Confidential* – to protect staff and those who complain

- *Informative* – providing information to management so that services can be improved

- *Simple* to understand and use

- *Fair* – with a full procedure for investigations

- *Effective* – dealing with all points raised and providing suitable remedies

- Regularly *monitored and audited* – to make sure that is is effective and improved.

Surveys undertaken by MORI in 1994 and 1997 (Page, 1997) to ascertain the public view of local authority complaint handling reveal that speed of response and good communications regarding the progress of complaints are valued most highly. Although specifically addressing public sector complaints, these, and the following points which emerged from these surveys, are highly salient:

- The attitude of complaints handling staff is most important – complaining is made more difficult by unhelpful staff.

- The public are not convinced that complaints are dealt with objectively.

- It is important that information regarding how to complain, and who to complain to, is clear and accessible.

- It may be inevitable that the complaints process is going to be lengthy in order to be fair to all parties, but this should be explained at the outset.

- More written explanations are required to account for decisions.

- Apologies have a major effect on how complainants view an investigation.

- Appeals procedures should be better publicised and explained.

A taxonomy such as that shown in Table 7:3 can be helpful both to members of the profession, to potential clients and to those who are dealing with complaints and discipline. Procedures for dealing with service complaints can be different, and more streamlined, than those for dealing with misconduct, and penalties will often be different.

7.6 New forms of support for complaints and disciplinary procedures

About a quarter of respondents to the PARN 2006 survey (24% of UK respondents and 29% of Irish respondents) affirmed that they had a client service charter, or similar public statement, setting out the standards of service that clients, customers, or patients should expect from professional service providers in their profession. This question was not asked in the 2003 surveys.

Table 7:3 Taxonomy of complaint types

EXTERNAL – brought by client, public, employer, or member of profession		INTERNAL – brought by profession or member of profession
Service	**Misconduct**	**Always misconduct**
Failure to deal professionally (client).* Failure to deal professionally (employer).* Failure to deal professionally (public).* Lack of professional competence (bad work – minor or one-off offence).	Failure to deal professionally (client).** Failure to deal professionally (employer).** Failure to deal professionally (public).** Lack of professional competence (bad work – major case of incompetence or series of offences that could bring the profession into disrepute). Inappropriate behaviour Failure to deal professionally (other professions).***	Misrepresenting qualifications to gain entry. Cheating in exams. Failure to maintain CPD. Failure to deal professionally (other professions).**** Failure to respond to professional body. Health (including substance abuse, mental health). Criminal conviction.

*   e.g. maladministration, communication
**   e.g. conflicts of interests, breaching confidentiality
***   e.g. failure to hand on information to superseding professional
**** e.g. poaching clients

- Chapter 8 -
Conclusions and recommendations

8.1 Conclusions

We distinguish ethical competence as a stage beyond technical competence. We also distinguish competence as a stage beyond competencies, and all these concepts as stages beyond what could be mistaken for all that is required of professionals; that is knowledge of the theory and techniques associated with a particular profession underlain by the capabilities to learn, the disposition to succeed in that type of profession and the motivation to succeed in this endeavour. Why? Because on one hand, we agree with government policy that what is taught in higher and further education is insufficient to succeed in the real world of work and, we would add, particularly not in the real world of professional practice. On the other hand we disagree with the thrust of government policy of the recent past, towards professional 'skills', which has been predicated on the assumption that the accumulation of specific functional competencies is sufficient for competence in all work including professional competence. Within the sector skills initiatives, for example, here has been no clear recognition of a distinction between employer-determined competencies required of lower level employees, which may be based on employer-perceived core competencies of their organisations, and professional competence that is shaped by a combination of all stakeholder perceptions of what is required by professionals, including employers as well as clients and the general public, but which is interpreted by, and supported by, professional associations.

Professional competence requires a range of technical and ethical competencies and for professionals to be able to 'put them all together' appropriately. Not only must professionals be able to call up, from a broad repertoire, competency in the particular techniques that will 'work', in the sense of doing what is expected of them technically (technical competence), but also they must be able to do what is 'right' ethically, which involves recognising an ethically sensitive situation and possibly forbearing from using certain techniques within their competence, as well as delivering whatever technical service is required in an ethical, or ethically sensitive, manner.

As noted in Chapter 4, the stages to ethical competence may not always be achieved in the order we have specified. Individuals are continually developing their learning capabilities and both dispositions and motivations change throughout our lives. New theories, techniques and competencies can be acquired through continuing professional development as well as during initial professional qualifications. Ethical competencies can be acquired before technical competencies. A newly qualified professional should be ethically competent even though technical competence may develop further in time. However, we believe it is important to recognise that ethical competence must build on a certain degree of technical competence, a certain repertoire of technical competencies, even if these will be added to in future. Without the stage of ethical competence there is a danger that professionalism will be mistaken for mere expertise. We believe that this association of professionalism with pure expertise has been detrimental to the professions.

We are not so naïve as to presume that all professionals are ethically competent. We have noted the widespread belief that the blind trust that most members of the public had for most of the traditional professions in the past has been replaced by a more cautious attitude. Trust must be earned, even if there may be a predisposition to give most traditional professionals the benefit of the doubt. It is important that these traditional professions provide evidence to the general public, and particularly to potential and actual clients/patients that practitioners are ethically competent. In addition we have noted that there are many occupations that have embarked on professionalisation projects. The picture of the professions today embraces occupational groups having achieved a wide range of degrees of professionalisation. Most professional associations representing these newly professionalising occupations are developing their professionalisation projects by specifically emphasising supports for the ethical competence of their practitioners. We believe these supports are essential for all professions, that professionalisation is an accomplishment that needs continual maintenance and development if it is not to whither and lead to a fall in trust in the practitioners of that occupation. This applies to traditional as well as new professions.

However the *manner* in which these supports are exercised is also important for the professionalisation of different occupations. A consequence of the decline in blind trust in the professions is that supports for ethical competence provided by professional associations must not be regarded as purely an internal affair of those professional groups. Clients/patients of professionals, potential clients/patients, as well as other stakeholders and the general public need to see that professional associations take seriously incidents of practitioners who do not exercise ethical competence. There are other ways that professional associations can, and do, support the ethical competence of their members. Having an Ethical Code is an obvious signal that an occupation association has moved along the path of professionalisation. However the codes need to be accessible to the public. In addition, as we have described in Chapter 5, there is a range of quality of Ethical Codes and a range of supports for the Ethical Code that professional associations can implement. These activities need to be implemented, and implemented in a manner that is also visible to the general public. In addition ensuring that ethics education is part of initial professional qualifications and that education and training in ethical competence continues for qualified members after qualification is important. This too needs to be in evidence to the general public.

In addition to encouraging greater awareness of ethical competence as a stage beyond technical competence, this book is intended to encourage professional associations to consider their support of the ethical competence of their members as a multifaceted process that involves many different policies. Some of these policies involve the more conventional complaints and disciplinary procedures and design of Ethical Codes, others are concerned with education, which for many has been limited to supporting technical competence. In addition a strategic or reflective attitude is needed concerning the effectiveness of these processes and policies. The quality and accessibility of codes, the incorporation of the latest theories and technologies in education practice must be reflected in materials devoted to ethical competence. Complaints and disciplinary procedures should be regularly reviewed and new currents of thought concerning good practice should be incorporated, such as the involvement of lay people and making the consequences of these procedures more public (and even the procedures themselves). In all we recommend that reflective practice among those running professional associations, or what we have called elsewhere the professionalisation of professional associations, should apply to this aspect of their activities. In addition a more reflective attitude towards how this area of professional association activity is presented beyond the membership is required. In all we conclude and recommend that supports for ethical competence should be considered at the highest, most strategic levels within professional associations.

8.2 Recommendations

8.1.1 Broad recommendations

Strategy
Consideration of ethical competence should move up from the ethics committee or the professional standards committee to become a regular concern of the governing bodies and of the top executive or executive groups in professional associations.

Supports for the ethical competence of members and their effectiveness need to be considered as a whole, rather than merely as individual activities or policies. Different types of support for ethical competence can still be designed and maintained in specific departments or by different individuals. Education specialists can develop those supports for ethical competence, specific committees to redesign the Ethical Code can be set up, complaints and disciplinary procedures will still be carried out by specialist groups, particularly supported by legal expertise. However the top level in the association needs to regularly consider the overall effectiveness of these efforts on the ethical competence of the membership.

Accessibility and Publicity
Remedial supports for professional ethical competence in the form of complaints and disciplinary procedures must be made more accessible to the wider public, not only in terms of communication but also through involvement of people other than members of the profession in those procedures. Positive supports for the ethical competence carried out by professional associations should also be communicated to clients and the wider public.

Lack of appreciation of other ways professional associations are supporting the ethical competence of their members encourages a view among members of the public that all there is to support ethical competence of professionals are complaints and disciplinary procedures. The closed manner in which these procedures have been pursued have also encouraged a public attitude that these procedures are window dressing, put in place to protect the professionals rather than to protect the public.

It is important that those whose technical or ethical competence has been found not to be up to the standards set by the profession, are being dealt with. The public wants to be assured that professional associations are either removing the right of such individuals to call themselves members of the relevant professional body, or to be assured that those individuals will improve their practice. If the mass media is taken as an indicator of public opinion, it seems that most would prefer to see that punishments are meted out involving expulsions in preference to remedial activities undertaken. This attitude encourages a view that the primary role of professional bodies in supporting the ethical competence of their members is to remove those that do not perform to standard, and perhaps to mete out punishments as a demonstration that technical and ethical competence will not be tolerated. This is encouraged by a lack of information concerning what professional associations are doing to support the ethical competence of their members in other areas such as education, training and ensuring that the code is up-to-date and of high quality.

8.2.2   Specific recommendations

- Ethical Codes should include reference to maintaining and developing competence and associations should consider a specific obligation to pursue continuing professional development and to support the continuing professional development of others in the profession. This latter element may be important as professional associations move towards output measures of CPD, which involve peer review. In the past PARN has recommended output measures of CPD be considered in preference to input measures.

- Ethical Codes should be regularly reviewed with a view to revision.

- When revising the code:

  o A wide range of codes from other professions should be consulted, possibly guided by the PARN 'Matrix' model.

  o Principles of good code design should be considered including clarity, consistency and comprehensiveness.

- The process of revising the code should involve as many of the members as possible. Widespread consultation over a considerable period of time should be considered.

- Contributions to ideas for how to revise the code should be open to a wider set of stakeholders than the membership, including specific invitations to associated professions as well as employers and also to clients and the general public through wider publicity.

- Ethics should form a clear component of all initial professional qualifications programmes.

- Continuing professional development programmes should include specific events and materials on the Ethical Code and guidelines to the code, on ethical dilemmas and other ethics materials (such as recent cases of disciplinary action taken by the association or relevant regulatory body).

- Continuing professional development policies should be consistent. If the policy is mandatory or compulsory, sanctions should be in place for non-compliance.

- Information on ethical issues should figure prominently in communications to members, and particularly on association websites. Consideration should be given to:

    - Guidance notes

    - Examples of ethical dilemmas

    - Advertisements for courses and seminars on ethics subjects.

- Ethics advice should be available. This can be through telephone helplines or through designation of particular individuals or committees that can be approached when members need advice. Smaller associations in related professions could consider pooling resources to provide this service collectively.

- Associations should encourage members and outside experts to write articles on ethical subjects for association newsletters and journals.

- Codes should be accessible to the public. We recommend:

- A clear path to the code from association website home pages preferably involving only one or two 'clicks'.

- Leaflets or other hard copy forms of the code should be available for clients and members of the public.

- In dealing with clients, such as in contracts, members of the profession should be obligated to refer specifically to the code or to include a copy of the code or precisely how to access it.

- Information regarding how to complain, and who to complaint to should be clear and accessible.

- Complaints handling staff should be trained to be helpful to those making complaints. This can involve:

  - Ensuring that they are pleasant and willing to listen to complainants during the initial encounter

  - Providing them with a set of stages that the complaint will go through to convey to the complainant at the outset including information about how likely the whole process is likely to take

  - Developing systems that the staff can use in order to inform complainants as to what stage in the process their complaint has reached.

- More written explanations are required to account for decisions.

- Appeals procedures should be better publicised and explained.

- Lay people should be involved in complaints and disciplinary procedures and they should form at least a substantial minority of those involved (at least a third). It is important that the practitioners do not swamp the lay people.

- There ought to be some form of support for the lay people.

- Findings should be made public. Some associations are doing this as can be seen from some of the case studies. This will admittedly cause some anxiety among those running professional associations, however we believe it is better in the long run for the reputation of the profession.

- A wide range of penalties should be available to disciplinary committees in addition to expulsion, suspension and issuing warnings. It is important that detailed investigations of disciplinary cases are undertaken and that justice is both done, and is seen to be done. It is therefore necessary that the "punishment fits the crime". In order for this to be achieved a wide range of punishments must be available. These could include:

  o Naming and shaming

  o Public apology

  o Fines paid to the association

  o Fines paid to the complainant

  o Re-education possibly through extra CPD requirements

  o Re-examination

  o Removal of privileges and particularly loss of status level such as fellowship or other degradation.

- The range of penalties available should be made public.

8.3   A final comment

There is much that professional associations can do to encourage and support the ethical competence of practitioners. We have come up with a long list of recommendations. However we would emphasise that these recommendations are based on good and interesting practice that already exists in the overall 'sector' of professional associations. As with other issues PARN has researched, there is a wide range of practice among professional associations. More associations need to learn of what others are doing to raise the overall level of support for ethical competence of their members and what others are doing to inform the public of these activities. More associations need to reflect on these practices in a strategic manner and to raise the level of their support for ethical competence, not only by copying what others are doing, but also by developing new forms of 'interesting practice' in this area. We believe that treating support of ethical competence as among the highest strategic issues for professional associations will make a significant contribution to encouraging, maintaining and restoring trust in particular professions, as well as the professional services sector as a whole, and that progress in this direction will be of enormous benefit to the public at large.

Appendix

- Appendix -
Empirical base

A.1 Introduction

We provide evidence for support for ethical competence provided by professional associations in the UK and Ireland based primarily on two sets of surveys carried out in 2003 and 2006. We report the results of these surveys as indicating the situation of the whole 'sector' of professional associations.[20] The quality of our generalisations to create statements describing the professional association sector depends on how:

- Comprehensive is the PARN database of information on the population of professional associations?

- Representative of the population of associations is the sample of survey respondents?

- Clear were the questions asked, how well were they understood?

- Accurately do the responses reflect the reality at each association?

All of these factors are issues common to the validity claims for any survey results. We do not claim that the information in this book provides a perfect view of the state of support for ethical competence among professional associations in the UK and Ireland in 2006, and we know it can be improved. However, we do claim that it provides the most comprehensive view of this aspect of the sector ever produced in the UK or Ireland.

---

[20] See Friedman with Afitska, 2007, Chapter 3 for a discussion of professional associations in the UK and Ireland as a sector.

A.2   Responses

Between April and July 2006 110 useable responses were received to the 334 questionnaires sent out as part of the 2006 PARN survey into the Professionalisation of Professional Associations in the UK. A similar survey was sent to 114 professional associations in Ireland in June and by December 2006, 21 useable responses were received. These surveys are being replicated in Canada and Australia and responses to these surveys will be compared with material published here in publications that will appear later in 2007.

The 2006 surveys build on comparable surveys carried out in 2003 in the UK and Ireland. Several questions have been altered, some questions have been added and some dropped, reflecting the development of our knowledge of the sector at PARN and reactions to the answers given in 2003. Where the questions were the same in both surveys, comparisons for the group of associations that responded to those questions in both surveys are provided.

The 2003 UK survey was sent to 299 professional associations and 129 useable responses were received while the 2003 Irish survey was sent to 114 professional associations and 25 useable responses were received. There were 61 professional associations that responded to both the 2003 and the 2006 surveys in the UK and 15 responded to both in Ireland.

A.3   PARN database

PARN regularly carries out exercises to 'prove' its database by telephoning to ensure that email addresses and names of associations are correct and keeping track of changes in the sector due to mergers, as well as collecting information about the size of associations and assigning them to 'industry' sectors. It is more difficult to keep track of new associations and break-away organisations, which are continually arising. We therefore would caution the reader that the estimation of the population of associations from our database will less comprehensively represent the actual population for the smallest professional associations (those with under 1000 members).

A.4   Representivity

We received 112 responses to the UK survey representing a 34% response rate. We rejected 2 of the responses based on them being purely trade associations. The 21 responses to the Irish survey, all of which were accepted as professional associations, represents a 18% response rate. This lower response rate reflects PARN's more recent presence in Ireland. Tables A:1 and A:3 provide information on the difference in size and sector between samples and population for the UK and Irish surveys.

Table A:1 Size of professional associations: UK vs Ireland

	Number of individual members					
	1-500	501-1500	1501-5000	5001-20000	>20000	Total
UK sample	8%	14%	28%	27%	23%	102[1]
UK population	7%	11%	32%	32%	19%	255[2]
Irish sample	16%	37%	37%	11%	0%	19[3]
Irish population	23%	32%	29%	14%	3%	66[4]

[1] Difference from 110 due to non response to the question about number of individual members.
[2] Difference from 334 due to lack of information about number of individual members.
[3] Difference from 21 due to non response to the question about number of individual members.
[4] Difference from 114 due to lack of information about number of individual members.

A.5   (Sub)Sector of respondents compared with population (sub)sectors

A.5.1   Sector distribution for respondents

Eighteen sectors were specified and respondents were asked to tick the one which best described the field of expertise that their association represents. The sectors were offered in alphabetical order. These are displayed in Table A:2 in grouped order. The second column, 'Detailed sector', shows the set of 17 possible 'sectors' offered in the questionnaire. The final sector offered was 'other'. The allocation of respondents to these sectors indicated by the respondents themselves was used, unless they chose 'other'. The 3 associations that chose other were allocated to specified sectors by PARN. The 'Group sector' column was assembled based on our understanding of how associations would group themselves.

Table A:2 Sector distribution of the sample: UK and Ireland

Group sector	Detailed sector	% Detailed UK	% Group UK	% Group Ireland
	Medical/health	21%		
	Public services	5%		
	Welfare/social	2%		
Health & social			28%	23%
	Accountancy	7%		
	Business/management	11%		
	Finance	6%		
	Law	1%		
	Marketing/PR	3%		
Finance, law business & management			29%	31%
	Agriculture/environment	7%		
	Engineering	11%		
	Science	6%		
	Surveying/construction	5%		
	IT/communications	2%		
Engineering, science, environment & construction			31%	31%
	Media/publishing	2%		
	Arts/creative	2%		
	Culture/leisure	3%		
	Teaching/academia	6%		
Education, media & culture			12%	15%

The three main sectors for the professions have been grouped and represent fairly equal proportions of the sample, that is, Health & Social; Finance, Law, Business & Management; Engineering, Science, Environment & Construction. The fourth group is more diverse, covering Education, Media & Culture. The UK and Irish samples are remarkably similar in the distribution across the 4 group sectors. Therefore differences in average responses between the two country samples are not likely to reflect sectoral differences among respondents.

Table A:3 Broad (sub)sector distribution of respondents compared with the population: UK vs Ireland

	Health & social	Finance, law, business, management	Engineering, science, environment, construction	Education, media, communi-cations, arts	Total
UK sample	27%	29%	30%	14%	110
UK population	28%	28%	28%	16%	334
Irish sample	24%	29%	33%	14%	21
Irish population	27%	27%	33%	12%	114

A.6 Clarity of survey questions

All questions from the 2003 surveys were reviewed in the light of how well they were answered. Minor adjustments were made to some questions, some were dropped and new ones added. In addition the questionnaire was reviewed by a small number of PARN members. This has been repeated as the survey has gone into different national versions. The questionnaire is still not 'perfect' in that some questions have been answered inconsistently by some respondents and some have been misinterpreted by some respondents. Generally when this has occurred these answers have been re-coded as non-responses.

A.7 Quality of responses

The surveys that were returned were of reasonably high quality, given that the questionnaire was long and that questions were wide ranging. One consequence of this is that it would have been difficult for a single person to answer all questions accurately (for large associations) unless they consulted colleagues or unless several individuals from respondent associations filled out sections of the survey that called upon their specialist knowledge of how the association operates. This requires considerable good will and effort from the person to whom the survey was sent in the first instance.

PARN identifies a primary contact at all of its members and attempts to identify a potential primary contact at non-members on the database. In many instances the primary contact at a non-member association will be familiar with PARN through attending PARN conferences and workshops and/or through purchasing PARN books. The questionnaire was sent directly to these people, rather than to the associations without a named contact.

The level of non-responses was fairly low for such a complex and long questionnaire, on average there were 8.5 or 6% of no responses over the 148 questions in the questionnaire.

A.8 Case studies

Case study material has been gathered through telephone interviews carried out with associations based on information given in the surveys, particularly prompted by answers to qualitative questions in the questionnaire.

Bibliography

Bibliography

Abbott A. (1988) *The System of the Professions*, Chicago, IL: University of Chicago Press.

Akerlof G.A. (1970) 'The Market for Lemons: Quality Uncertainty and the Market Mechanism', *The Quarterly Journal of Economics*, 84, 488—500.

Allen M. (1993) *A Conceptual Model of Transferable Personal Skills*, Sheffield: Department of Employment.

Anscombe G.E.M. (1958) 'Modern Moral Philosophy', *Philosophy*, 33, 1-19.

Aristotle. (384-322 BC/1999) *Nichomanchean Ethics* (2nd ed.) Indianapolis, IN: Hackett Publishing Company.

Beauchamp T.L. and Bowie N.E. (2004) *Ethical Theory and Business*, (7th ed.), London: Pearson Education.

Boyatzis R.E. (1982) *The Competent Manager: A Model for Effective Performance*, New York: Wiley.

Cabinet Office (1998), *How to deal with complaints*, web-page at http://www.servicefirst.gov.uk/1998/complaint/bk5top10.htm.

Carr D. (2005) 'Personal and Interpersonal Relationships in Education and Teaching: a Virtue Ethical Perspective', *British Journal or Educational Studies*, 53:3, 255-271.

Chappell C., Gonczi A. and Hager P. (2000) 'Competency-based Education', in Foley G. (ed.) *Understanding Adult Education and Training*, (2nd ed) London: Allen & Unwin, 191-205.

Cheetham G. and Chivers G. (2005) *Professions, Competence and Informal Learning*, Cheltenham, UK: Edward Elgar.

Dale M. and Iles P. (1992) *Assessing Management Skills: a Guide to Competencies and Evaluation Techniques*, London: Kogan Page.

Dearing R. (1996) *Review of Qualifications for 16-19 Year Olds,* London: Schools and Curriculum Authority.

Eraut M. (1994) *Developing Professional Knowledge and Competence,* London: Falmer.

Field L. (2000) 'Organisational Learning: Basic Concepts', in Foley G. (ed.) *Understanding Adult Education and Training,* (2nd ed) London: Allen & Unwin, 34-58.

Flanagan O. (1991) *Varieties of Moral Personality, Ethics and Psychological Realism,* Cambridge, MA: Harvard University Press.

Flanagan O. (1996) *Self Expressions: Mind, Morals and the Meaning of Life,* Oxford: Oxford University Press.

Freedman M. (1975) *Lawyers' Ethics in an Adversary System,* Indianapolis, IN: Bobs-Merrill.

Friedman A.L. (1994) 'The Information Technology Field: Using Fields and Paradigms for Analyzing Technological Change', *Human Relations,* 47/4, 367-392.

Friedman A. (ed.) (2005) *Critical Issues in CPD,* Bristol: PARN.

Friedman A.L. (2006) 'Strengthening Professionalism: Ethical Competence as a Path Towards the Public Good', in Craig J. (ed.) *Production Values: Futures for Professionalism,* London: DEMOS, 104-110.

Friedman A. with Afitska N. (2007) *Professionalism and Sustainability in the Professional Associations Sector: UK and Ireland,* Bristol: PARN.

Friedman A., Daly S. and Andrzejewska R. (2005) *Analysing Ethical Codes of UK Professional Bodies,* Bristol: PARN.

Friedman A., Durkin C., Davis K. and Phillips M. (2000) *Continuing Professional Development in the UK: Policies and Programmes,* Bristol: PARN.

Friedman A.L. and Miles S. (2001) 'Socially Responsible Investment and Corporate Social and Environmental Reporting in the UK: an

Exploratory Study' *British Accounting Review*, 33:4, December, 523-548.

Friedman A., Phillips M. and Timlett R. (2002) *The Ethical Codes of UK Professional Associations*, Bristol: PARN.

Gert B. (2004) *Common Morality: Deciding What to Do*, Oxford: Oxford University Press.

Gonzi A., Hagar P. and Athanasou J. (1993) *The Development of Competency-based Assessment Strategies for the Professions*, (Research Paper No 8), Canberra: Australian National Office of Overseas Skills Recognition.

Hackett S. (2001) 'Educating for Competency and Reflective Practice: Fostering a Conjoint Approach in Education and Training', *Journal of Workplace Learning*, 13:3, 103-112.

Hursthouse R. (1999) *On Virtue Ethics*, Oxford: Oxford University Press.

Jones C. (2005) 'Character, Virtue and Physical Education', *European Physical Education Review*, 11:2, 139-151.

Kohlberg L. (1981) *Essays on Moral Development. Vol 1. The Philosophy of Moral Development,* San Francisco, CA: Harper and Row.

Kolb D.A. (1984) *Experiential Learning: Experience as The Source of Learning and Development*, Englewood Cliffs, New Jersey: Prentice-Hall.

Larson M.L. (1977) *The Rise of the Professions: a Sociological Analysis*, Berkeley, California: University of California Press.

Marshall K. (1991) 'NVQs: An Assessment of the Outcomes Approach to Education and Training', *Journal of Further and Higher Education*, 15:3, 56-64.

Mason P. (1982) *The English Gentleman*, London: Andre Deutsch.

McGaghie W.C. (1993) 'Evaluating Competence for Professional Practice', in Curry L. and Wergin J.F. (eds.) *Educating Professionals*, San Francisco: Jossey-Bass, 229-61.

Messick S. (1984) 'The Psychology of Educational Measurement', *Journal of Educational Measurement*, 21, 215-38.

Mill J.S. (1863) *Utilitarianism*, New York: Library of Liberal Arts 1957 [originally published in three parts in *Fraser's Magazine*, 1861, and entire as a book, 1863].

Murphy B. and Otter S. (1999) 'A common Sense Issue', *Times Higher Education Supplement*, August 6.

NAB/UGC (National Advisory Board for Public Sector Education/University Grants Committee) (1984) *Higher Education and the Needs of Society*, London: NAB.

Neuberger J. (2006) *The Moral State We're In*, London: Harper Perennial.

O'Connor A. and Hyde A. (2005) 'Teaching Reflection to Nursing Students: a Qualitative Study in an Irish Context', *Innovations in Education and Teaching International*, 42:4, 291-303.

Page, B. (1997) 'Complaints: Handle with Care', *Customer Service Management*, December, 28-29.

Peters T. and Waterman R. (1982) *In Search of Excellence*. New York: Harper and Row.

Pithers R.T. (1998). *Improving Learning through Effective Training*, Katoomba, Aust: Social Science Press.

Prahalad C.K. and Hamel G. (1990) 'The Core Competence of the Corporation', *Harvard Business Review*, 68:3, 79-90.

Pritchard M.S. (2006) *Professional Integrity: Thinking Ethically*, Lawrence, Kansas: University Press of Kansas.

Puka B. (1999) 'Inclusive Moral Education: a Critique and Integration of Competing Approaches', in Leicester M., Modgil C. and Modgil S. (eds.) *Moral Education and Pluralism*, London: Falmer Press.

Reece S. (2002) *Can the Professions Survive?* London: Royal Society for the Encouragement of Arts, Manufactures & Commerce.

Rylatt A. and Lohan K. (1995) *Creating Training Miracles*, Hemel Hempstead, UK: Prentice Hall.

Sartre J-P. (1957) 'Existentialism is a Humanism', (trans Mairet P.) in Kaufmann W. (ed.) *Existentialism from Dostoevsky to Sartre*, New York: Meridian, 287-311.

Schmiedinger B., Valentin K. and Stephan E. (2005) 'Competence Based Business Development – Organizational Competencies as Basis for Successful Companies', *Journal of Universal Knowledge Management*, 1, 13-20.

Schön D.A. (1983) *The Reflective Practitioner: How Professionals Think in Action*, London: Maurice Temple Smith.

Smith D., Wolstencroft T. and Southern J. (1989) 'Personal Transferable Skills and the Job Demands on Graduates', *Journal of European Industrial Training*, 13:8, 25-31.

Styron W. *Sophie's Choice*, New York: Bantam Books.

Taylor F.W. (1911 orig 1967) *The Principles of Scientific Management*, New York: W.W. Norton and Co.

Wilensky Harold L. (1964) 'The Professionalisation of Everyone?' *American Journal of Sociology*, 70/2, 137-158.

Woodruffe C. (1990) *Assessment Centres: Identifying and Developing Competence*, London: Institute of Personnel Management.

About PARN Publications

Professional Associations Research Network

The Professional Associations Research Network (PARN) is a membership organisation dedicated to the support of good practice among professional bodies.

This book is one of many titles available from PARN. A list of titles and the topics covered can be found on our website along with an order form: www.parn.org.uk

RELATED TITLES:

The Ethical Codes of UK Professional Associations.
By Andrew Friedman, Mary Phillips and Rose Timlett
This book presents an overview of current codes of conduct. It examines their purpose, structure and content, as well as the range of stakeholders to whom professional obligation might be due. It also provides preliminary ideas as to how codes might be enforced. The book will facilitate benchmarking between professional associations and offers food for thought for those revising their ethical regulatory structures or processes. The analysis is based on data collected during between 2000-01 and at a PARN workshop in February 2002.

2002 – paperback – 82 pages – ISBN 0-9538347-7-8

Analysing Ethical Codes of UK Professional Bodies.
By Andrew Friedman, Sasha Daly and Ruth Andrzejewska
This is the second book on professional ethics produced by PARN. At the heart of the book is an innovative research tool. This ethical 'Matrix' can be used to help evaluate professional codes in terms of the clarity, relative emphasis, and appropriateness of particular statements within codes, and also in terms of the coverage of obligations and stakeholders in particular codes compared with an overall 'map' of values and stakeholders.

2005 – paperback – 117 pages – ISBN 0-9545487-3-6

Other PARN Publications:

<u>In the CPD Series:</u>

Critical Issues in CPD (2005)
Continuing Professional Development in the UK: Evaluation of Good Practice (2002)
Continuing Professional Development in the UK: Attitudes and Experiences of Practitioners (2001)
Building CPD Networks on the Internet (1999)

<u>In the Governance Series:</u>

Governance of Professional Associations: Theory and Practice (2006)
Governance of Professional Associations: The Players and Processes (2003)
Governance of Professional Associations: The Structure and Role of the Governing Body (2002)

<u>On Membership:</u>

Member Relations and Strategy: Supporting Member Involvement and Retention (2006)
Analysing Member Services: A Strategic Perspective for Professional Associations (2003)
Membership Structures of UK Professional Associations (2002)

<u>Also:</u>
Professionalism and Sustainability in the Professional Associations Sector: UK and Ireland (2007)
Professional Associations in Ireland: A Comparative Study with the UK (2004)
The Professionalisation of UK Professional Associations: Governance, Management and Member Relations (2004)

A NEW TITLE 'THE GROWING PAINS OF SMALLER PROFESSIONAL ASSOCIATIONS: KEY ISSUES AND INTERESTING PRACTICE' WILL BE PUBLISHED IN JUNE 2007

To order PARN publications, visit our website: www.parn.org.uk.